THE CATECHIST FORMATION BOOK

Growing & Sharing

REV. DAVID A. SORK
DON BOYD
SR. MARUJA SEDANO

PAULIST PRESS — *New York/Ramsey*

Acknowledgements
   The publisher wishes to gratefully acknowledge the use of the following materials:
   Excerpt from Free and Faithful in Christ, Vol. I *by Bernard Haring, copyright © 1978 by the author, used by permission of The Crossroad Publishing Company.*
   Excerpt from A Curriculum Guide for Continuous Progress in Religious Education, *used by permission of N.C.E.A.*
   Excerpt from "A Vision of the Church as Mother of the Poor" *by Jeff Dietrich, used with permission of Catholic Agitator.*
   Excerpt from Not Without Parables *by Catherine de Hueck Doherty. Copyright © 1977 by Ave Maria Press, Notre Dame, Indiana 46556. Used with permission of the publisher.*

Photo Credits
   Vernon Sigl: 5, 7
   Vivienne della Grotta: 28, 163
   Vera Wulf: 48, 181
   Pat Agre: 62
   Kay Freeman: 77
   David S. Strickler: 97
   Paul S. Conklin: 117
   Wendell Rideout: 147
   Paul M. Schrock: 149

Nihil Obstat
Joseph Pollard, S.T.D.
Censor Deputatus

Imprimatur
Timothy Cardinal Manning
Archbishop of Los Angeles
November 24, 1980

The *nihil obstat* and *imprimatur* are official declarations that a book or pamphlet is free of doctrinal or moral error. No implication is contained therein that those who have granted the *nihil obstat* and *imprimatur* agree with the contents, opinions or statements expressed.

Copyright © 1981 by
David A. Sork

All rights reserved. No part of this book may be reproduced or transmitted in any form or by any means, electronic or mechanical, including photocopying, recording or by any information storage and retrieval system without permission in writing from the publisher.

Library of Congress
Catalog Card Number: 80-84507

ISBN: 0-8091-2365-7

Published by Paulist Press
545 Island Road, Ramsey, N.J. 07446

Printed and bound in the
United States of America

CONTENTS

INTRODUCTION 1

PART ONE: CATECHIST IN FORMATION

UNIT ONE—GOD UNFOLDS HIMSELF THROUGH THE AGES 7
    PREFACE TO PART ONE 7
1. CONCEPT OF GOD 10
2. CONTEMPORARY CONCEPT OF REVELATION 15
3. SCRIPTURE AND TRADITION 24

UNIT TWO—CHRIST: THE FULLNESS OF REVELATION 28
1. THE GOSPEL'S UNDERSTANDING OF JESUS 28
2. THE APOSTLES' AND THE CHURCH'S GROWING UNDERSTANDING OF JESUS 33
3. THE INCARNATION: THE HUMANITY OF CHRIST 36
4. THE INCARNATION: THE ROLE OF MARY 40
5. JESUS CHRIST THE SACRAMENT OF GOD 45

UNIT THREE—COMMUNITY OF FAITH 48
1. FORMATION OF COMMUNITY AS PEOPLE OF FAITH 48
2. CHURCH AS PEOPLE OF GOD 51
3. CHURCH AS SACRAMENT OF CHRIST 54
4. LITURGY: PUBLIC CELEBRATION OF THE FAITH COMMUNITY 57

UNIT FOUR—INITIATION INTO THE COMMUNITY OF FAITH 62
1. THE SACRAMENTS OF INITIATION 62
2. BAPTISM 65

3. CONFIRMATION 70
4. EUCHARIST 72

UNIT FIVE—DEVELOPMENT OF THE PERSON 77
1. STAGES OF GROWTH AND OF READINESS FOR THE MESSAGE 77
2. SACRAMENTS OF COMMITMENT 86

UNIT SIX—GOD'S CALL: OUR RESPONSE 97
1. GRACE: THE PRESENCE OF GOD 97
2. LIFE OF GRACE: ACCEPTANCE OR REJECTION 101
3. MORALITY 107
4. CONSCIENCE FORMATION 112

UNIT SEVEN— WE ENCOUNTER GOD THROUGH OTHERS 117
1. THE PROPHETS AND THEIR SOCIAL MESSAGE 117
2. COMMUNAL NATURE OF SIN 123
3. CATHOLIC TEACHING ON SOCIAL JUSTICE 127
4. SACRAMENTS OF HEALING 134

PART TWO—CATECHIST AS TEACHER

UNIT ONE—DEVELOPMENT OF THE LESSON 149
PREFACE TO PART TWO 149
1. EXPLORATION OF LESSON PLANNING 150
2. MODELS OF LESSON PLANS 154
3. EXPERIENCE OF THE CATECHIST VERSUS THE STUDENT 157
4. APPLICATION OF EXPERIENCE TO MESSAGE 160

UNIT TWO—THE LEARNING SITUATION 163
1. A LOOK AT LEARNERS 163
2. ASSESSMENT OF NEEDS 165
3. TECHNIQUES FOR MOTIVATION 168
4. COPING WITH THE STUDENTS 170
5. CREATING A CONDUCIVE SETTING 173
6. PARENT INVOLVEMENT 176

UNIT THREE—PROCESSES FOR LEARNING 181
1. ADAPTATION OF MATERIALS FOR THE STUDENT 181
2. PROJECTS FOR VARIOUS AGE LEVELS 183

INTRODUCTION

The title of this book summarizes its orientation and direction. Growing signifies something in process. Sharing signifies involvement and interaction. In his apostolic exhortation, "Catechesi Tradendae," Pope John Paul II says that we are all to be catechized. Our growth in faith is a lifelong process. And sharing one's faith is the call extended to all Christians. So, in a broad sense, we are all catechists.

This book evolved out of a most rewarding ministry. For over ten years we have been actively involved in preparing catechists through catechist formation courses sponsored by the Los Angeles Archdiocesan Office of Religious Education. In that decade we have seen a number of significant changes develop in these courses as religious education itself was evolving. The very change in name from "teacher training" to "catechist formation" tells much of the story.

This book is not the Los Angeles program. Rather, it is a development from our cumulative experiences of offering catechist formation courses in both Spanish and English. It was certainly written with some of our former catechist-learners in mind. Some live in the inner city, others in the suburbs, still others in the barrios. They include people with Ph.D.'s, and some with a sixth grade education. They comprise a variety of racial and ethnic groups. (In one course we gave three years ago, the learners included Anglos, Samoans, blacks, Chicanos, and Filipinos.) Because of the variety of learners and teachers, no course is ever the

1

same. While no book can meet the needs of all, we have tried to design it with a certain flexibility to the various persons who may be reading it.

A person may have been teaching for many years yet still not be prepared to be a catechist. A teacher imparts facts to students so that they might increase their knowledge or acquire certain skills. What people teach is not necessarily an intimate part of their lives. A person may even be merely a *teacher* of religion where religion is seen as another subject to be taught.

On the other hand, a catechist is more than a teacher. Catechists are called to share their faith-life with the learners. A catechist wishes the whole person to grow from within and to be changed. What a catechist teaches is not something "out there" but within. The faith-life of a catechist has much to do with how effective the catechist is. Who the catechist is, indeed, is much more important than what the catechist does or knows. The National Catechetical Directory says:

> As important as it is that a catechist have a clear understanding of the teaching of Christ and his Church, that is not enough. He or she must also receive and respond to a ministerial call, which comes from the Lord and is articulated in the local church by the bishop. The response to this call includes willingness to give time and talent, not only to catechizing others, but to one's own continued growth in faith and understanding (NCD 206)

Although a teacher of religion could conceivably be an atheist, a catechist is necessarily a person of faith. The National Catechetical Directory goes on to describe the qualities of a catechist. He or she is a witness to the Gospel (NCD 207), a proclaimer of the message as presented by the teaching authority of the Church (NCD 208), a sharer in community (NCD 209), and a servant of the community (NCD 210). A catechist formation course should prepare adult learners to look at themselves in light of these personal religious qualities as part of the formation process.

The purpose of catechesis is to deepen one's faith in a closer communion with Jesus Christ. Although growth in knowledge is an important aspect of catechesis, if the learning process does not engender growth in faith, it is not effective catechesis. On graded-level programs, the vast majority of catechetical textbooks use an experiential approach to catechesis. Concerning experiential catechesis the National Catechetical Directory says:

> Catechists should encourage people to reflect on their significant experiences and respond to God's presence there. Sometimes they will provide appropriate experiences. They should seek to reach the whole person, using both cognitive (intellectual) and affective (emotional) techniques. (NCD 176)

It is our conviction that if a catechist is to teach experientially, he or she must experience, first-hand, experiential catechesis. Therefore, the thrust of a catechist formation course should be experiential, not academic. This book has been designed to facilitate for both the teacher (master catechist) and the catechist-learners the experiential approach. The person should look at one's life-experience to see where he or she has encountered God and reflect on that experience in light of the Christian message. The doctrine of the Church is in reality the authoritative expression of the reflections of the cumulative life-experiences of that community of faith which we call the Church. The magisterium of the Church is the authoritative guide to guarantee that these reflections are faithful to the basic message of salvation. But all Christian believers are part of that reflective process. In "Catechesi Tradendae," Pope John Paul II says:

> Authentic catechesis is always an orderly and systematic initiation into the revelation that God has given of himself to humanity in Christ Jesus, a revelation stored in the depths of the Church's memory and in sacred Scripture, and constantly communicated from one generation to the next by a living, active *traditio*. This revelation is not however isolated from life or artificially juxtaposed to it. It is concerned with the ultimate meaning of life and it illumines the whole of life with the light of the Gospel, to inspire it or to question it.
>
> That is why we can apply to catechists an expression used by the Second Vatican Council with special reference to priests: "instructors of the human being and his life in the faith." (art. 22)

Too often people come into a catechist formation course looking for the right technique to communicate the theme of the next week's lesson. Were the teacher of the formation course to design it in such a "band-aid" approach which only answers a catechist's most immediate, felt need, the catechist may end up missing the point of catechesis. In order to communicate their faith to others, catechists must know what their faith is. To know doctrinal formulation is not sufficient if catechists have not integrated it into their lives and are not able to articulate it in terms of their life experience.

The book is divided into two parts: "Catechist in Formation" and "Catechist as Teacher." The second part should not be dealt with until after the first part is completed. The aim of the first part is to bring the adult learner to an understanding of the teachings of the Church through an experiential approach. In this way it enables a growth in faith to take place in the learners and it helps them to articulate their personal faith. The aim of the second part is to help the learners communicate that faith to others whom they are called to catechize. This should not be seen as a doctrine/methods dichotomy. For even in the first part, the very means by which the message is communicated should be a model for the catechist-learners of good methodology. Catechesis involves an integration of doctrine with the means by which that doctrine is communicated. The learners should see this means of communicating the message as effective not because it is good for their potential learners but because they have personally experienced in the catechist formation course that it was effective in developing their own faith.

It is our hope that if taught effectively, this book will help people to be good catechists not just because they have learned the skills and competencies of sharing effectively the faith but primarily because their own faith has deepened as they have been growing and sharing in formation as a catechist.

Part One

CATECHIST IN FORMATION

Unit One

GOD UNFOLDS HIMSELF THROUGH THE AGES

PREFACE TO PART ONE

Any good teacher begins with the self-admonition not to presume too much. Before going too far into this book, we feel that it is important to be sure that the potential catechist is sufficiently familiar with the "tools of the trade" before proceeding any further. The basic source for any catechist is the Holy Bible. The catechist without at least a rudimentary knowledge of how to use the Bible is at a distinct disadvantage.

A person should first know how to find a particular passage in the Bible. Originally there was not a particular order or sequence of all the books of the Bible. Our arrangement here will follow the order of the Catholic *New American Bible*. This is not to imply that it is the best arrangement. It is just one arrangement. Since this particular version is the translation most Catholics hear on Sundays, it was chosen for this book.

Each of the seventy-three books found in the Bible is divided up into chapters and verses. Although the division is arbitrary and was done only within the last one thousand years, it is recognized by all and does facilitate finding the Scripture passage. If one saw the passage Jn 1:4, this would mean the first chapter of the Gospel according to St. John, verse 4: "Whatever came to be in him, found life, life for the light of men." However, if you saw the passage 1 Jn 1:4, this would mean the first chapter of the first letter of St. John, verse 4: "Indeed, our purpose in writing you this is that our joy may be complete"—a totally different passage! Since there are three letters attributed to St. John as well as a Gospel, this can be a source of confusion.

The chart is meant to simplify the location of a particular book among the seventy-three in the Bible. The books are listed according to how they appear in the *New American Bible*.

The threefold division is meant to be a memory-serving tool more than anything else. Didactic means instructive. Although one might question how, for example, the Book of Psalms would be considered instructive, it falls into that category more than into an historical or prophetic one. Some books of the Bible are known by different names according to the version of one's Bible. Possible alternate designations are indicated on the chart in parentheses. Seven of the books in the Old Testament are marked with an asterisk. These books were only recognized as part of the Bible by the Jews of Alexandria because they were written in Greek, not Hebrew. Catholics consider these seven books as part of the Bible; Protestants, in general, do not. These books are often called the Apocrypha ("hidden" or "spurious") or the deutero-canonical books.

The books designated as Paul's community letters are those letters which were written by Paul to the Christian Church of a particular city. For example, "Romans" would refer to the letter Paul wrote to the Church living in Rome. The books designated as Paul's pastoral letters are those written by Paul to a particular person. For example, 1 Timothy would refer to the first letter Paul wrote to his friend Timothy. The catholic letters are those circular letters sent around to the different Christian communities. For example, "Jude" would refer to that circular letter written by St. Jude to be read by all the Christian communities.

For practice, see how well you can locate the following passages:

Jer 31:31–34
Mt 25:31–40
3 Jn 1:11–12
Ex 20:1–17
Ps 23
Sir 26:1–4

OLD TESTAMENT

	BOOK	ABBREVIATION	CHAPTERS
Historical Books			
Pentateuch	Genesis	Gn	50
or	Exodus	Ex	40
Torah	Leviticus	Lv	27
	Numbers	Nm	21
	Deuteronomy	Dt	34
	Joshua	Jos	24
	Judges	Jgs	21
	Ruth	Ru	4
	1 Samuel (1 Kings)	1 Sm	31
	2 Samuel (2 Kings)	2 Sm	24
	1 Kings (3 Kings)	1 Kg	22
	2 Kings (4 Kings)	2 Kg	25
	1 Chronicles	1 Chr	29
	2 Chronicles	2 Chr	36
	Ezra (1 Esdras)	Ezr	10
	Nehemiah (2 Esdras)	Neh	13
	Tobit*	Tb	14
	Judith*	Jdt	16
	Esther	Est	10
	1 Maccabees*	1 Mc	16
	2 Maccabees*	2 Mc	15
Didactic Books	Job	Jb	42
	Psalms	Ps(s)	150
	Proverbs	Prv	31
	Ecclesiastes (Qoheleth)	Eccl	12
	Song of Songs (of Solomon)	Sg	8
	Wisdom*	Wis	19
	Sirach (Ecclesiasticus)*	Sir	51
Prophetic Books	Isaiah	Is	66
	Jeremiah	Jer	52
	Lamentations	Lam	5
	Baruch*	Bar	6
	Ezekiel	Ez	48
	Daniel	Dn	14
	Hosea	Hos	14
	Joel	Jl	4
	Amos	Am	9
	Obadiah	Ob	1
	Jonah	Jon	4
	Micah	Mi	7
	Nahum	Na	3
	Habakkuk	Hb	3
	Zephaniah	Zep	3
	Haggai	Hg	2
	Zechariah	Zec	14
	Malachi	Mal	3

NEW TESTAMENT

	BOOK	ABBREVIATION	CHAPTERS
Historical Books	Matthew	Mt	28
	Mark	Mk	16
	Luke	Lk	24
	John	Jn	21
	Acts of the Apostles	Acts	28
Didactic Books			
Paul's	Romans	Rom	16
Community	1 Corinthians	1 Cor	16
Letters	2 Corinthians	2 Cor	13
	Galatians	Gal	6
	Ephesians	Eph	6
	Philippians	Phil	4
	Colossians	Col	4
	1 Thessalonians	1 Thes	5
	2 Thessalonians	2 Thes	3
Paul's	1 Timothy	1 Tim	6
Pastoral	2 Timothy	2 Tim	4
Letters	Titus	Ti	3
	Philemon	Phlm	1
	Hebrews	Heb	13
Catholic	James	Jas	5
Letters	1 Peter	1 Pt	5
	2 Peter	2 Pt	3
	1 John	1 Jn	5
	2 John	2 Jn	1
	3 John	3 Jn	1
Prophetic Book	Revelation (Apocalypse)	Rv	22

9

1. CONCEPT OF GOD

A catechist is more than a teacher. A teacher imparts facts to students so that they may increase knowledge or acquire certain skills. The subject of a teacher can very easily be something outside of the teacher's life: something "out there." But a catechist is sharing personal faith-experience with his or her learners and wishes the whole person to grow and to be changed. The subject matter is not something "out there" but is rather "within."

Your faith life will have much to do with what kind of a catechist you are. Who you are is much more important than what you can do. The first thing you should consider as a prospective catechist is your own concept of God. Your idea of God and your relationship to God determines who you are as a catechist. Your message to your students about God flows from how you see God. If your own teacher (master catechist) in this program understands and appreciates your idea of God, he or she will be able to meet your needs in this course more effectively.

Not all have the same vision of God. Others in your class or parish will have concepts of God different from yours. If you can appreciate the differing ideas of God, you yourself will be enriched in your awareness of God. God is much wider and infinitely greater than any single idea. When you are teaching, your students will have different concepts of God, depending on where they come from and who have touched their lives.

This section hopes to address this issue. One's culture, age, family, etc., affect one's image of God. We shall try to show how this has taken place in the past and is taking place today. It is hoped that an understanding and appreciation of that will enable you to see how the influence of others has helped and still helps you form your image of God.

Perhaps the section of the Old Testament most familiar to the reader is the account of creation. Actually one does not find one account but two (Gn 1:1–2:4a; and 2:4b–25). Although these two accounts of creation appear side by side in the Bible, they were actually written by different persons reflecting different cultures and ages. Because of that, the two accounts give us different concepts of God. We will compare the two to see how the different backgrounds of the two authors have influenced their respective concepts of God.

The author of Genesis 1:1–2:4a wrote at a very bleak moment in the history of Israel: the Babylonian captivity (587–539 B.C.). The high points of Israel's history were long past. A series of tragedies in rapid succession had seen the destruction of the holy city Jerusalem and the temple, the end of the dynasty of the kings of Judah, and the mass deportation of the leaders and some of the people into Babylon. For many it seemed as if God had abandoned Israel. She now lived in the midst of a pagan and polytheistic people. These exiles desperately needed a sense of identity as well as a continued feeling of destiny as a people. Their God had to be seen in marked contrast to those other gods.

To maintain her identity Israel had to be set apart from any other nation and its cult. Since Israel no longer had a land to claim as her own, her source of unity was not as a kingdom but as a worshiping community. Therefore, the author of this section of Genesis presents the history of Israel in a liturgical setting.

Read Gen 1:1–2:4a

The events describing creation are presented to anticipate the creation of Israel as a worshiping community. The eight acts of creation are compressed into six days so that the Lord may rest on the sabbath, for Jewish law required that the sabbath be a day of rest. The account of creation was written to be in sharp contrast with the creation story of the Babylonians. God is considered the sole origin of all creation. Even the pagan deities are seen in Genesis as themselves works of God's creation. The pagan world said that the gods consulted among themselves, and then one of them created man. Genesis says that God consulted with himself before creating man. Man is seen as surpassing all other creatures because of his relationship to God. Male and female were created together, both in God's image.

It is appropriate here to comment that the account of creation was never intended to be a scientific treatise. The author of Genesis knew no more about creation than any other person living at that time. The six days of creation have nothing to do with six billion years or six epochs. The author's purpose was religious, not scientific. He wanted these dejected Israelites in Babylon to know that the same God who did so much for them in past history, who set up a covenant with them in ages past, and whom they are to worship as a people, is the same God who created all things including the deities of the Babylonians.

In comparison, there is the second account of creation (Gen 2:4b–25). The author wrote at a much brighter period in Israel's history than existed at the other account: the glorious reign of King Solomon, son of David (965–926). The kingdom of Israel was never more powerful. It was only at this time, during the reigns of David and Solomon, that both the northern and the southern kingdoms were united. There was, however, a concern that, with all her temporal power, Israel would forget her destiny to be a people ruled by God, not man. Israel needed to realize that the monarchy in Israel was no accident, but a part of God's plan.

Read Gen 2:4b–25

In this account God is seen as someone very close to man. The personal name Yahweh ("He-who-is") is used, the name which God used in identifying himself to Moses. God is manlike. He is pictured as a potter forming man out of clay. Woman is described as being formed from the side of man. This much more intimate and anthropomorphic idea of God arose because the people really did feel close to God at this time in history. They had a powerful king, and their country was as strong as it had ever been in history. They had a place of worship: the temple. Their identity as a people was clear. The theme in this section on good and evil was emphasized because the author feared that Israel might evolve into just another secular kingdom like some of the surrounding nations. These nations were the personification of evil. A faithful Israel was the personification of good. Israel must remain faithful to Yahweh, so that Yahweh might work through her.

We now turn from these cultures found in Genesis to some more recent peoples and cultures. Like the peoples in these two creation accounts, these people also held their concept of God because of who they were and where they were coming from.

The culture of Hispanic America is rooted in the ancient civilizations of the Incas of Peru, the Mayas of Central America, and the Aztecs of Mexico. The God-Creator held very little importance to them, for he passed on various assignments to lesser deities. These were the ones who really controlled the destinies of individuals and nations. Humans were not responsible for their actions. Everything was determined by outside forces. Religion and destiny ruled their lives.

Famine, war, sickness or any other misfortune was seen as a sign of the anger of the gods. For sheer survival man had to placate these deities. The people would offer to the gods sacrifices of food, animals, and even human hearts.

God the Father was a very cold, distant power. The people's relationships were to these lesser deities, often called sons of God. These ones were their friends. They protected the people and even gave their lives for them. The female deities were connected with the earth and fertility. When the Spaniards came and conquered the Indians, they felt that their male gods had betrayed them. The people then turned to their female deities for veneration. This probably is why the Latin American has such a deep devotion to Mary, the mother of God.

Considering the people's impersonal image of the God-Creator, it is not surprising that during colonial times the concept of God for the Latin American people was that of an authority figure. God was a stranger who defeated their own gods and conquered their lands. He was powerful and punishing.

Religion, politics, and culture have strongly conditioned Latin Americans to be a passive people who are powerless to change the world. Although this concept is still held, the Latin American is coming to a different understanding of God and with it to a different world-view. Many of the people today no longer view fatalistically their situation of alienation, misery, and exploitation. The situation is the result of a system which can and should be changed. They must take the responsibility to determine their destinies.

Liberation theology presents to the Latin American a new image of God: a God who sent his only Son, Jesus, to deliver them not only from the slavery of sin but also from those conditions of oppression and exploitation. God is personal, near, and interested in their well-being. He desires a just world and wishes to lead the people to a new state of freedom.

Black Americans came to this country involuntarily as slaves. With their induction into a slave ethic, they were stripped of their personal and social identity as a people of worth. In this new environment, blacks were treated as less than human. They had no rights. Their only acknowledged worth was what was reflected on them by virtue of the esteem, wealth, and power of their white masters. The most important virtue instilled in them was subservience. Still, there were some blacks who talked a different line. Either because they were new to this continent or because they had received the carefully preserved traditions of their ancestors, they related stories of their African culture and their history as a free people. However, after several generations of born slaves, many of these stories of freedom were seen more as a legend than as history. Such tales were viewed with disdain by most slaves, who had decided to make the best of their lot. Many came to a belief in a God who asked blacks to wait, to temper their anger, and to absorb their pain without retaliation. They saw their slavery in the same light as did the white culture which benefited from it: it was simply the way God wanted it.

As the economic, political and social systems of slavery began to fall, so did the rationales and justifications that perpetrated it. American blacks began to formulate different understandings of themselves and of their condition. They began to validate their worth internally rather than by the external standards of another culture. They began to develop pride in their blackness and the triumph and development in a world which offered them little.

With the black community there have developed two contrasting images of God. The first is of a God who still asks that they wait and that they make no parallels between what is social and what is religious. Others, however, reject this image of God as being an opiate for blacks to perpetuate servitude to the dominant culture. Their image of God is that of God the liberator. For these the prophetic call is heard in the messages of the Martin Luther Kings and the James Cones. Much as God delivered the Israelites from the slavery of the Egyptians, God is calling blacks to respond to him. This God is one who calls to the black masses to throw off the bonds of values that distort a healthy wholeness for the black American.

Although it is presumptuous to generalize about a country as heterogeneous as America, one can find certain American cultural characteristics. During the nineteenth century the United States of America saw its boundaries extend from the Atlantic to the Pacific. Vast areas of the continent were added to the country by purchase, stealth, and wars. Pioneers set out toward uncharted lands to claim as their own. It was the era of the rugged individualist. In economics the thoughts of Adam Smith and laissez-faire capitalism predominated. The barons of big business transformed America into an industrial giant. On the international level America acquired territory in the Caribbean and the Pacific. Invoking the Monroe Doctrine she assumed the role of the protector of Latin America. The central theme running through America was "Manifest Destiny."

The American image of God was one who has bestowed special favors on this country. The wealth of America was a sign that God predestined her for this special role. America was the new Israel. On the level of the individual, wealth and success were signs of a person's special destiny for salvation. The virtues arising out of such an image of God are thrift, sound investment, and industry. Wealth then comes only to the moral man. There was little, if any, sense of community responsibility. It was a "God-and-me" covenant rather than "God-and-us." The prophets of such a God were people like the Rockefellers, the Carnegies, and the Morgans.

None of these ideas of God is complete. Some give a better vision of God than others. As we examine our own concept of God, we must always relate it to the Scriptures. Is there a contradiction between our idea of God and what the Scriptures say? Has our culture and background hampered or enhanced our understanding of God? A series of photographs of someone taken from different angles gives a more complete picture of the person than just one photograph. So it is with Scripture. One passage of Scripture gives only one view of God. But as we see different passages of Scripture, a more comprehensive vision of God comes forth.

Read the following passages. What images of God do they give you?

Is 49:8–26
Jer 31:1–22
Ps 22:1–32
Ps 23:1–6
Wis 11:21–26
Mt 11:25–30
Acts 17:22–31

QUESTIONS FOR REFLECTION

1. What was your image of God when you were a child? _____
_____
_____
_____
_____

2. What is your image of God today? _____
_____
_____
_____
_____

3. What events do you think helped your image of God mature? _____
_____
_____
_____
_____

2. CONTEMPORARY CONCEPT OF REVELATION

It is basic to our Judaeo-Christian tradition that God has revealed himself to us in time. Ours is an historical religion. As believers we accept God's revelation as a fact. Now we need to ask how God does it. God is an invisible, spiritual reality. To describe God in human terms is always a woefully inadequate task, but it is the only way we can describe him. And the only way God can manifest himself to us is through material creation. Thomas Aquinas once said we know more about what God is not than about what he is. So how does God tell us about himself?

God can only reveal himself to us through things we perceive, our everyday experiences. Since revelation takes place in history, God must deal with us through the events and experiences with which we are familiar. Let us go back to the roots of our religion to see just how God has done this.

For our ancient ancestors covenants were formal agreements by which men related to one another in society. Agreements were outwardly manifested by some ritual such as cutting an animal in half and having the two parties walk between them. This public ceremony was seen as part of this covenant or formal agreement. In Genesis 31 Jacob made a covenant or pact with his father-in-law, Laban. They agreed on territory and possessions, built a mound of stones as a memorial of this agreement and had a meal together to solemnize it. Conditions of the pact were laid down, and both swore to it.

God wished to reveal to us that he is one who cares about us and wishes to enter into a relationship with us. He is one who is very much part of history. God made himself known through the very covenants by which people in Israelite society entered into relationship with one another. Even the rituals God used were the same. God did not invent these covenants; he simply adapted pre-existing ones for his purposes.

There are found in the Scriptures many covenants which God made with some of his people: e.g., Adam (Gn 2), Noah (Gn 9), and Abraham (Gn 12; 15; 17; 18). But the covenant that really climaxes Jewish salvation history is the covenant of Sinai. When Christians speak of the old covenant, they are speaking of the covenant of Sinai (Ex 19f).

What exactly was the Sinai experience? Somehow, in some way, God communicated himself to Moses, thereby intervening in history in a unique way. It was a communication that made Moses realize that God was intervening in their lives in a way completely different from any other tribe or nation. This revelation needed to be communicated to the people in terms which they could understand.

Different covenants were already in use at the time of the Sinai experience. An extremely close parallel to the Sinai covenant has been found in the Hittite capital—a treaty or legal agreement made between the Hittite king and his vassals. Its purpose was to provide mutual support for both parties. The pact was unilateral: the king himself was not bound. In return for his oath of obedience to the king, however, the vassal could put complete trust in the king's good will that the king would protect him from foreign aggressors. It is often referred to as the Hittite suzerainty pact.

Point by point the parallel between that pact and the Sinai covenant is uncanny. In the Sinai covenant each of the tribes of Israel was both subject to Yahweh and bound to each other. No tribe was sovereign, and the terms of the covenant allowed each tribe to govern its own internal affairs without interference as long as the religious obligations of the covenant were observed.

Realizing that this Sinai covenant paralleled existing suzerainty pacts, the people understood clearly their relationship to Yahweh. Their covenant was not a contract worked out through tough bargaining by two sides. It was rather the result of the free initiative of an all-powerful God who bound this chosen people to himself in obedience and fidelity. The very term "covenant fidelity," *hesed* in Hebrew, is so rich that no word in English can adequately convey its meaning. It connotes that love, that mercy, that infinite generosity and patience by which God has bound himself to us. He has done so not out of legal obligation but out of his complete goodness. God was loyal to the covenant even when the people were not. On the people's part *hesed* describes that person who in his or her own way shared in that quality which God manifested. The love between David and his friend Jonathan was *hesed*. All good Israelites were called to have this covenant virtue toward God and one another.

To fail to understand covenant and all its implications is to misunderstand what God's revelation meant. It was precisely because covenants were common formal agreements by which people established relationships with one another that God's relationship to his people came through covenants. They could encounter God through experiences already familiar to them. The Sinai covenant was the key to opening the channels of communication between God and his people. All Israelite history both before and after was seen in view of the Sinai experience. Their relationship to God and their understanding of him came by means of covenant language and thought patterns.

God chose ordinary people to be the instruments of his revelation. The prophets give us several examples of this, but let's concentrate on a couple of them: Amos and Hosea. The two were contemporaries, and both preached fidelity to the covenant around the eighth century B.C.

At the time of Amos there were two kingdoms of Israelite tribes: Israel in the north and Judah in the south. Amos was a shepherd from Tekoa, an obscure village of the kingdom of Judah. His ministry was to the kingdom of Israel. Amos' very words tell us of his humble origins but divine mission:

> I was no prophet, nor have I belonged to a company of prophets; I was
> a shepherd and a dresser of sycamores. The Lord took me from following the flock, and said to me, Go, prophesy to my people Israel (Am 7:14–15).

The Book of Amos describes four visions that indicate his mission to the north. The visions follow the cycle of the seasons. The first vision came in the spring and the fourth one in the fall. Amos used everyday experiences to reveal the message: the swarm of locusts (7:1–3), the fire (7:4–6), the plumb line (7:7–9), and the basket of ripe fruit (8:1–2). These visions of destruction announced the punishment of Israel. What is of interest here is not so much the message, but how the message was communicated. Through his humble spokesperson, Amos, God used the ordinary events of people's lives to reveal their covenant responsibility. The people's relationship with Yahweh had been disintegrating, and Amos came to tell them that.

> What phenomena of nature might we use today to express our relationship with God? What experiences tell us a similar message?

How was it that a man as simple and uneducated as Amos could even conceive of delivering a message of doom to the sophisticated Israelites of the north? Amos himself was a man of deep faith. He had a close relationship to Yahweh. He lived the covenant to the fullest. He experienced an inner compulsion by God to announce the impending destruction to Israel, a compulsion that overcame Amos' own natural unwillingness and his feeling of his own unworthiness. What won out in the end was Amos' deep faith in and complete obedience to God.

The prophet Hosea, unlike Amos, was from the north. He also saw Israel falling away from the covenant. Like Amos he denounced the crimes of Israel. Hosea used another everyday event of people's lives to reveal God's message to Israel: the marriage relationship. Hosea was involved in a tragic marriage to Gomer, who played the part of a harlot. Her adulteries did not cause Hosea to reject her. His love was ever abiding. He used the tragedy of that story as an analogy for Israel, who was unfaithful to God and the covenant which God formed with her. Yet despite Israel's unfaithfulness, the love of God perdured. There is perhaps no more forceful way of describing how loving and forgiving God is than through such a story. No extraordinary vision or miraculous sign was needed. Just a simple love story.

> Can you think of a similar story that could communicate that quality of God—something that could really move your learners?

Many religions recognize these events described above as God's revelation. Where religions differ is in how that revelation is interpreted and what it means for today. Religions agree that revelation still occurs today, but they differ as to how it occurs.

Recently an announcement came from David Spencer, the spiritual leader of the Mormon Church. He said that he had received a revelation from God. The message was that the time was now ready for black men to be admitted into the priesthood of the Church. Until this revelation came, all blacks were excluded from the Mormon priesthood because they were said to have the mark of Cain on their foreheads. According to Mormon doctrine no man-made law, public vote, or external pressure could change that teaching. Such a change could come through a new revelation from God. And this revelation finally came.

That's the Mormon view on divine revelation. Often when we hear the word "revelation," we might think of the Book of Revelation, the last book in the Bible. Because of our association of revelation with that book, our idea of revelation may include elements such as mystical language, strange symbols, cryptic messages, forecasts of impending doom, extraordinary miracles, angelic messengers, and visions of Mary or one of the saints.

The concept of revelation in the eyes of the Catholic Church is much broader than this. Revelation would be the words and events by which God makes known himself and the mystery of his will. The *Constitution on Divine Revelation* of the Second Vatican Council says:

> By this revelation, then, the invisible God, from the fullness of his love, addresses men as his friends, and moves among them, in order to invite and receive them into his company. This economy of revelation is realized by deeds and words, which are intrinsically bound up with each other. As a result, the works performed by God in the history of salvation show forth and bear out the doctrine and realities signified by the words; the words, for their part, proclaim the works and bring to light the mystery they contain (n. 2).

Revelation does not come primarily through extraordinary visions or magical writings but through the ordinary events of our lives. Writing to the Romans St. Paul says: "Whatever can be known about God is clear.... He himself has made it so. Since the creation of the world, invisible realities, God's eternal power and divinity, have become visible, recognized through the things he has made" (Rom 1:19–20).

In the section on the concept of God, we were really examining the process of revelation. We saw how events and situations affected people's ideas of God. The two accounts of creation showed us that even the Bible looks at God from different views. In more recent times, events and situations determined how some of the cultures around us view God. Hopefully, we were able to see how we ourselves came to an idea of God. Those words and events which colored our idea of God were themselves part of the revelation process.

Revelation is both complete and ongoing. On the one hand, no new public revelation is to take place until the second coming of Christ. Christ himself is the fullness of revelation. In Christ is everything which the Father has to reveal to us. We can know no more about the Father than what Christ has revealed in himself. On the other hand, God is still unfolding the mystery of himself and his divine will through the events of today. The National Catechetical Directory refers to the former sense as "revelation" and to the latter sense as "manifestation" or "communication" (n. 50). The ongoing events of history help us to understand more clearly what is God's revelation. To interpret these events in light of Christ is the task of us, the Church. Vatican Council II's *Constitution on the Church in the Modern World* says:

> At all times the Church carries the responsibility of reading the signs of the time and of interpreting them in the light of the Gospel if it is

to carry out its task. In language intelligible to every generation, she should be able to answer the ever recurring questions which men ask about the meaning of the present life and of the life to come, and how one is related to the other. We must be aware of and understand the aspirations, the yearnings, and the often dramatic features of the world in which we live (n. 4).

Reviewing the events of the Old Testament shows us how God revealed himself in and through the ordinary events of people's lives. Since revelation is ongoing and, therefore, still taking place today, the process of revelation will be the same. God will reveal himself to us, and we will encounter God, through the ordinary events of our lives.

Very often in our search for God we are called to touch on happenings in our lives when God was made real. In most situations, this probably would have occurred through our relationships with parents, grandparents, or other members of the immediate family.

Think in your very own life the time you were first told about God.
How old were you?
Who was the person telling you?
Can you remember the circumstances, such as place or purpose?

In many instances we find that God was introduced to us as very small children. This most generally was done by a member of the family. It may have happened on a trip to church with the family. It could have happened at the knee of a grandparent teaching us prayers. It might have happened as a result of a death of a loved family member. The reasons would be unique to each of our family circumstances, but it most likely would have happened within the context of the family.

The God we were introduced to at that time would certainly have been vague to us. It might have been a good experience or one that was not very pleasant. It was, however, our first introduction. It was that initial awakening of something within us that started us on a lifelong search for more understanding and knowledge about God. It might even have included long periods of time taken out from our search, but there was always some awareness that there was more to discover.

So much of who God is to each of us today has been developed through our relationships with our parents or other significant adults in our lives. If we lived in a family where both parents showed us a lot of love and security, our awareness of God reflected that. If we lived in a broken family with only one parent yet with much love and affection, our awareness of God reflected that. Our parents' own idea of God and their relationship with him also revealed something of God to us. How our family expressed community and how they looked at others in society also affected how we perceived God's revelation. Our parents and family members in their unique and individual ways have revealed the Father to us. This is the history of our people, one generation revealing to another who God is.

The events of our early life naturally have a profound effect on how we experience God's revelation, but they aren't the only things. Often even in the twilight years of our life, God can reveal himself in a new way through a new experience. One such experience of God occurred to a man who was in that waning period of his life. And it occurred because a group of children cared enough about this man to make him see that he was a worthwhile person in the eyes of others.

A parish CCD class took part in a program of parish ministry to the aged. They were to send letters to parishioners confined to convalescent homes as well as pray for them each time the class met. A monthly newsletter was sent to all these individuals. One class in particular had sent a card and letter to a man who had been in a convalescent home for ten years. It arrived just two days before Thanksgiving. A few days after Thanksgiving the parish received from the man's wife the following letter:

> My husband has been a member of your parish for over forty years. He had just celebrated his 84th birthday on Thanksgiving Day. I was writing to speak to the teacher and class that wrote to my husband, telling him that they cared and were praying for him.
>
> I am 84 years old. With my advanced age I am no longer able to drive, so I took the bus twice each week to visit my husband. The day before Thanksgiving, Jim called me and asked me to come to see him that day. He was so excited and sounded so at peace. Although I had planned on being there on Thanksgiving Day, I responded to his call, caught the bus, and visited. He was very weak when I arrived. In his hand was a card. He took my hand and gave me the card. He was smiling as he told me about the kids that had been praying for him. He knew that someone in this busy world besides myself was reaching out in love and kindness to him.
>
> I am Lutheran, but my husband has been a good Catholic all his life. This is the first time that either of us can remember anyone caring. I called today to tell you my Jim died on Thanksgiving afternoon. I would like with all my heart to thank the teacher and those children who showed such kindness. Jim died knowing that he was loved very much. I can't say more but how grateful I am. God came to my Jim and me in a very special way. He came through the letters, cards, and prayers of people who care. Thank you.

Stories like this one could be repeated many times over by those people involved in that outreach program to the infirmed. People who have been away from the Church for many years have been touched in special ways. Families have called, written, and visited to thank the students and teachers. They experienced in one of the most vivid ways possible what it is to reveal the Father to others. Such events happen through the lives and experiences of others.

God's revelation to the Israelite people came as they reflected on their history and recalled certain high points or crises in their history. Our own lives are really marked by similar crises or high points. Crises that take place at different moments of our life can be a means of encountering God. Great conversion experiences have often sprung forth from a deep crisis in one's life. Paul's experience on the road to Damascus, Ignatius Loyola's experience in the monasteries of Montserrat and Manresa following his battlefield accident, Dorothy Day's conversion from communism to Christianity, Malcolm X's conversion to God following his prison experience: all these arose out of a crisis in their life.

Crises often bring people to a close union with God. For most of their lives God may have seemed remote, unreachable, and distant and was rarely, if ever, thought of. He was not part of the here-and-now world where they lived, worked, and grew. This does not imply that they were Godless people; it simply means that at that time God had taken a secondary place in their lives.

But then suddenly something happened. It may have been the birth of their child. They had seen young babies before. But this baby was their baby. They had conceived it. They had either felt or watched it grow. They had taken part in the process of this child coming from the protection of the womb into the world. The mystery of it all had brought them to a greater awareness and a sense of awe at the Divine. God's role in creation had never taken on such meaning as now.

Often it is a tragic crisis that brings one into contact with God. When a close relative is dying, we first may rely heavily on the expertise of those in the field of medicine. Our hope often is for a miracle drug, a successful surgery, a remission of the disease—anything that will make the loved one well. During this time, one may find oneself close to God, calling on him to cure the person, to take away the suffering, and ultimately to give the loved one peace.

Throughout our lives we can pinpoint crisis moments. They might include the first time we had to live on our own, the first time we felt love for the one we wished to live with the rest of our life, serious breaks in the relationships with loved ones, the serious illness of a child, change in jobs, or financial problems that affect our lives. They may simply be times when we are not able to come up with easy answers. These may often be the very times when we become closer to God or come to a greater awareness of who God is. These are times when God touches our lives in special ways. These are the events, just ordinary events, by which God reveals himself to us.

No new public revelation will take place until the second coming of Christ. In Christ is all there is to know about God. But as long as people are still alive, as long as history is recorded, as long as the ordinary events of people's lives still occur, we will be reflecting on God's revelation. Every new happening gives us an opportunity to reinterpret the meaning of God's revelation in light of these experiences. Each reflection then gives us an opportunity to come to a greater awareness of who God is and what it is he has revealed to us about himself through his Son, Jesus Christ.

> Write down an experience in your life in which you feel you revealed God to others.

By reflecting on *our* history, by viewing *our* story, by examining the ordinary events of *our* lives, we become part of a revelation people. As a revelation people, we have our collective history. We have a tradition that has been passed on, reflected upon, passed on again, and again reflected upon. Our reverence for the Scriptures arises out of our solidarity with this revelatory tradition passed down through the ages and put into writing through the inspiration of the Holy Spirit. Our respect for the doctrines of the Church arises out of our solidarity with the Church's reflections upon the events of our history passed on through the centuries. Revelation becomes most real when we are able to assimilate our own personal history in encountering God with the collective reflections of this believing community we call Church.

As a catechist you are a key figure in enabling revelation to come alive in your students. You are not called to give the students faith, but to enable their faith to grow. A catechist does not primarily impart doctrine. Church doctrine is the means by which the Church of a particular age formulated its reflections on revelation.

> Doctrine is not merely a matter for the intellect, but is the basis for a way of life as envisioned by St. Paul: "Let us profess the truth in love and grow to the full maturity of Christ the head" (Eph 4:15) (*To Teach As Jesus Did,* n. 20).

Rather than merely teaching the truths of the faith, catechists are catalysts trying to stimulate in the students a faith already present. As a catechist you are called to enable God's revelation to become alive in your students, and thus you should try to use the same process by which God revealed himself to us: take the life and experience of the students, allow them to reflect on it and to see God unfolding himself to them through it, and relate that reflection to the reflections of this believing community we call Church. Unless this is done—no matter what the age of the student, 7 or 70—all the dogmatic formulas, all the Scripture passages, and all the ready-made, memorized answers in the world will have no relevance to their life and faith. The approach that is modeled after God himself in his revelation to us is often called experiential catechesis.

QUESTIONS FOR REFLECTION

1. How has God taken the life experiences of his people in revealing himself in salvation history?_____

_____

2. How has Jesus addressed the life experiences of his listeners to whom he preached in his public ministry?

3. How has God touched your life and through what experiences have you encountered God's revelation?

4. How would you enable your learners to get in touch with God's revelation through their life experiences?

FORMATION OF THE PENTATEUCH

1800 B.C.   Abraham, patriarch of all. Story begins.

1250 B.C.   Moses' deliverance of the Israelite people to the frontier of the promised land. Oral accounts begin to develop into a story of a nation. Original legal code of Israelites began.

950 B.C.   Story of a nation put into writing for the first time: "J" document.

700s B.C.   Story of a nation as developed in the northern kingdom put into writing: "E" document.

722 B.C.   "E" document is brought south and is blended with "J."

700 B.C.   Priests who had come to Jerusalem from the north put their legal tradition into writing: "D" document.

500s B.C.   Legal traditions of the Jerusalem priesthood are put into writing: "P" document.

c480 B.C.   The editor of the "P" tradition puts that tradition into writing with the already blended JE document. "D" is added on.

3. SCRIPTURE AND TRADITION

The first five books of the Bible are known as the Pentateuch. (In Greek "pente" means "five" and "teuchos" means "book.") The Jews call this the "Torah" or Law. This is the most revered part of the Jewish Bible. Moses is ascribed as the author of these five books. A simplistic view of Mosaic authorship would say that Moses was inspired by God to write down the very words which we read today in the books of Genesis, Exodus, Leviticus, Numbers, and Deuteronomy. This would mean that, since Moses lived around the thirteenth century B.C., these books were written at that time.

Virtually all Scripture scholars today would deny such a simplistic statement of Mosaic authorship. In fact, by analyzing the writing style of the Pentateuch, scholars have found that there is not one author but many and that the Pentateuch was written over a period of hundreds of years. The final form as we have it today is the result of an editing process including both oral and written sources. While this book is not intended to be a Scripture course, understanding how the Pentateuch was formed is important for catechists, for if they know the formation process involved, they can see the relationship between Scripture and oral tradition. Knowing that, they will understand more clearly the process of revelation itself. Scripture then will not be seen as some magic mantra. Rather it will be seen as the written source of the growing faith life of a community as that community developed in its understanding of and relationship with God.

The mass media are such an integral part of our society that it is difficult to conceive of life without them. However, mass communication is a relatively recent phenomenon. Television is barely older than a generation, and radio is virtually unique to the twentieth century. Even the printing press is only about four hundred years old. Yet history has been recorded for thousands of years. For most of recorded history, the stories of people were passed on to succeeding generations without benefit of television, radio, newspapers, or, often, even written literature. People relied on their memory.

A family or tribe acquired its identity through the events and exploits of its ancestors. These stories were carefully told and retold from parent to child for generations. When there was no written literature or when practically everyone was illiterate, the family or tribe, rather than the printed word, was the medium of communication. This "passing on" by word of mouth of one's history is commonly called "oral tradition."

Although the Scriptures give us a history of the Israelite people dating back to the nineteenth century before Christ, the writings themselves are much more recent. Much of what we read about is taken from oral traditions. Stories such as those about Abraham, Isaac, and Jacob were passed down by word of mouth for hundreds of years before acquiring a written form. In Israelite society a particular family was assigned the important responsibility of preserving the tribal traditions. Children of the Israelite tribe were taken by their parents to this family, and this family would see that the children knew the stories verbatim. This family was considered *the* authority on anything to do with the Israelite traditions.

Although Abraham lived around the nineteenth century, the basic story of the Pentateuch apparently developed around the thirteenth century. At this time Moses led the people out of the land of Egypt, made the covenant with Yahweh on Mount Sinai, and handed on the leadership to Joshua, who finally led the people to the promised land. Inspired by Moses' leadership long after his death, generation after generation of Israelites passed on this narrative of the Israelite people by word of mouth. This oral tradition was not put into writing until the era of the kings—around the tenth century. This written literature is called the Jahwistic or "J" document because the author generally refers to God as Yahweh (or Jahweh).

After the death of Solomon in 926, the kingdom was divided into Israel and Judah. Another narrative of the Israelite nation was developed by the northern kingdom (Israel) and was put into writing around the eighth century. This written literature is called the Elohistic or "E" document because the author generally refers to God as Elohim.

In 722 the northern kingdom was conquered by the Assyrians. Not wishing to lose the story of their national heritage, the Israelites of the north brought the "E" document south to Judah where it eventually blended in with the "J" document. It was also at this time that the priests who had come from Israel put their oral legal traditions into a written legal code, a second law to the original Sinai covenant. This written literature is known as the Deuteronomic or "D" document. (In Greek "deutero" means "second" and "nomos" means law.) It is seen in its most complete form in the Book of Deuteronomy.

The legal traditions of the priests of the southern kingdom Judah were put into written form around the sixth century. This written literature is known as the Priestly or "P" document. Although it is the newest of the written documents, it contains perhaps the oldest of the oral sources handed down faithfully through the ages. The "P" tradition was at this time blended by this southern editor into the already blended "JE" document. The "D" document was added to all this. So what we have in the Pentateuch today is a combination of the four Mosaic traditions "JEPD" along with some other additions.

The "J" and the "E" are two different renditions of the history of a people led toward the promised land by Moses. The two legal codes were drawn up by the priests of the northern kingdom ("D") and the priests of the southern kingdom ("P"). Recognizing the Pentateuch as inspired by God, one should remember that all of this process of formation should be seen as no accident but as under the guidance of him who called these descendants of Abraham, Isaac, and Jacob to be a chosen people.

It should be no surprise then to find that there are certain discrepancies in the accounts of the Pentateuch. In each age the story of Israel was related according to the culture and times of the people; the laws were codified according to the culture and times of the people; the message of salvation was proclaimed according to the culture and times of the people. God uses his own people to make himself known to them. The message of salvation is unchanged. But as long as human beings are involved, it must be translated through the medium of these people. It's like the sun. The rays of the sun might all be the same, but its light is only appreciated as it is reflected in myriads of colors as the light bounces off different objects.

If one were to read in 1870 two different accounts of the Civil War, one by a northerner and one by a southerner, one would certainly see differing pictures of the same event. If the great grandchildren of these two individuals were to write today, there might still be a northern and southern version, but the differences would not be so obvious. Each author is still reflecting the culture and times of his people.

In the book of Genesis there are two different accounts of the creation of the world. 1:1—2:4a reflects the "P" tradition. 2:4b–25 reflects the "J" tradition. Read the two and compare. See if you can detect the differences.

Three ("J," "E" and "P") of the four major traditions are found in the Book of Genesis. In some places they have been so blended that it is impossible to tell which tradition is evident in a particular passage.

Exodus contains all four traditions. Leviticus contains only the "P" tradition. Numbers contains the same three traditions as Genesis. Deuteronomy contains almost exclusively the "D" tradition although there are a few scattered sections containing "J," "E" and "P." There is no need to go into these in detail, but rather than the details of the formation process, the catechist should keep in mind the principle behind it: namely, in revelation God uses the ordinary events in the lives of people to make himself known to his people.

QUESTIONS FOR REFLECTION

1. What are the traditions and customs that are important to the life and identity of your family? How are these preserved and handed on?

2. We have seen how the Pentateuch is the blending of traditions from several families or tribes. How have different traditions converged into your family?

3. Who are the key persons in your family who have enabled you to share and carry on these traditions? _____
_____
_____
_____
_____

4. What are the everyday events which have enabled you to know God more closely? _____
_____
_____
_____

Unit Two

CHRIST: THE FULLNESS OF REVELATION

1. THE GOSPELS' UNDERSTANDING OF JESUS

The Gospels represent the most accurate portrayal of who Jesus was and is. In our search to obtain an understanding of Jesus with authenticity, we must rely on the Gospels. Although other non-biblical records of Jesus do exist, they are extremely sparse. Without the Gospels we would have almost no knowledge of Jesus.

Even the Gospel accounts give us a limited image of Jesus. We do not know his size—whether he was tall or short. There is no record of the color of his hair, eyes or skin. Very little information exists regarding his family, and practically nothing is known of his youth. Matthew and Luke give us an account of his birth, and Luke records an incident when at twelve years of age Jesus is found in the temple (2:41–52). From there we move to the start of Jesus' public ministry at about thirty years of age when he is baptized in the River Jordan by John the Baptist.

In reading the Gospel accounts of the life of Jesus, it is important to keep in mind that they were not written specifically as an historical document or a biographical sketch of Jesus. They were, instead, the treasured memories of the words and works of Jesus that transformed the lives of people. Since the Gospels were written more than a generation after the death of Jesus, it is not surprising that Scripture scholars have found that many of the words attributed to Jesus are not necessarily a verbatim quote of what he actually said. They are often reflections of the disciples of Jesus. These followers heard and later recalled the message, reflected upon it, and then used it as a means of proclaiming Jesus to others. The message of Jesus lived on after his death through his disciples.

Jesus was conceived by the power of the Holy Spirit in the womb of a young girl named Mary, still a virgin but engaged to a man named Joseph. Mary and Joseph were married when the time had come for Jesus' birth. He was born in a manger in the town of Bethlehem. His parents lived their lives as Jews and reared Jesus in their Jewish faith. They had him circumcised after eight days and presented him in the temple after forty days in accordance with the Mosaic Law.

After Jesus' birth little is known about his childhood until he is twelve years old. Luke's Gospel does relate an incident about Jesus' being lost and found in the temple. Mary and Joseph were worried, concerned parents. They reacted in much the same way as parents would react today.

> "Son, why have you done this to us? You see that your father and I have been searching for you in sorrow." He said to them: "Why did you search for me? Did you not know that I had to be in my Father's house?" But they did not grasp what he said to them (Lk 2:48–50).

Luke comments that after the temple incident Jesus returned with them to Nazareth, lived obediently with them, and grew in wisdom, age, and favor before God and men. And that pretty much sums up what is known about Jesus' childhood.

Jesus began his public life with his baptism by John the Baptist in the River Jordan. In his baptism Jesus, fully human in all ways except sin, in obedience to his Father's will accepted in total freedom his role of the suffering servant (Mk 10:35; Lk 12:50). In Jesus' acceptance we find the roots of our redemption. The essence of redemption consists in Jesus' free, filial obedience to the Father.

In Jewish society during the time of Jesus it was customary for a person to select a rabbi or teacher. He would be taught by the rabbi, live with him, and imitate all that the rabbi had to teach. In so doing the person would master the ability to hand on the teachings of that rabbi to others. But Jesus was different. Unlike other rabbis or teachers, Jesus selected his disciples, not vice versa. He made the initiative.

A look at the Gospel accounts clearly shows us that the disciples did not understand Jesus. In fact, it is very unlikely that the disciples ever understood who Jesus was while he was alive. A fuller understanding had to await the enlightened vision of a post-resurrection faith. Mark relates some incidents indicating the disciples' misunderstandings:

> He began to teach them that the Son of Man had to suffer much, be rejected by the elders, the chief priests, and the scribes, be put to death, and rise three days later. He said these things quite openly. Peter then took him aside and began to remonstrate with him. At this he turned around and, eyeing the disciples, reprimanded Peter: "Get out of my sight, you satan! You are not judging by God's standards but by man's" (Mk 8:31–33).

He was teaching his disciples in this vein: "The Son of Man is going to be delivered into the hands of men who will put him to death; three days after his death he will rise." Though they failed to understand his words, they were afraid to question him (Mk 9:30–32).

Their misunderstanding was such that it even led to petty jealousy (Mk 9:33–37), fear, denial, and, finally, betrayal.

To some of his followers with whom Jesus developed a particularly close friendship he revealed his mission and vision of life. He would speak especially to the Twelve:

Now when he was away from the crowd, those present with the Twelve questioned him about the parables. He told them: "To you the mystery of the reign of God has been confided. To the others outside it is all presented in parables, so that they will look intently and not see, listen carefully and not understand, lest perhaps they repent and be forgiven" (Mk 4:10–12).

The disciples were on the road going up to Jerusalem, with Jesus walking in the lead. Their mood was one of wonderment, while that of those who followed was fear. Taking the Twelve aside once more, he began to tell them what was going to happen to him (Mk 10:32).

Jesus had a special relationship to the poor. Yet this relationship should be seen within the context of Jesus' announcement of the coming of the reign (kingdom) of God and the compassion and mercy of the Father. Through this message Jesus offered hope to the poor. When hope is offered to people who are hungry, downtrodden, or oppressed, it is readily received. When people are rich, well-fed, and self-sufficient, the message is not as readily heard. Jesus announced his mission when he stood up in the synagogue to read a passage from Isaiah:

"The spirit of the Lord is upon me; therefore, he has anointed me. He has sent me to bring glad tidings to the poor, to proclaim liberty to captives, recovery of sight to the blind and release to prisoners, to announce a year of favor from the Lord."

Rolling up the scroll he gave it back to the assistant and sat down. All in the synagogue had their eyes fixed on him. Then he began by saying to them: "Today this Scripture passage is fulfilled in your hearing" (Lk 4:18–21).

Luke's Gospel more than any of the others relates Jesus' care, concern, and ministry to the poor. Jesus praised the widow for the small donation she made to the temple out of the little she had (21:1–4). Jesus spoke of the difficulty of a rich man entering the kingdom of God (18:18–25), yet praised Zacchaeus for detaching himself from his wealth (19:1–9). Jesus told the followers of John the Baptist that Jesus had come to preach the good news to the poor (7:22) and told the Pharisees not to invite the wealthy to the feast but the beggars, blind, crippled, and lame (14:12–13). Jesus pronounced blessings on the poor (6:20) and woes on the rich (6:24).

Jesus preached to the people about the need for repentance because the reign was close at hand. The Greek word for repentance, "metanoia," implies a radical change, a complete reform or conversion. This radical change or conversion from within is at the core of the message of Jesus. He called people to the Father so that they might share in the kingdom. To reduce the Gospel message of Jesus to participation in social reform or any other cause would be a distortion or lack of understanding of Jesus. The life of Jesus exemplified what he has asked of us: a life of service and total obedience to God.

The Gospels show Jesus to be a man of prayer. We see him going off to the hills where he spent the whole night in prayer with God before selecting the Twelve (Lk 6:12–13), and he took along with him Peter, James, and John as he went up to the mountain to pray (Lk 9:28–29). Discussing prayer in common, Jesus says:

> "If two of you join your voices on earth to pray for anything, it shall be granted you by my Father in heaven. Where two or three are gathered in my name, there am I in their midst" (Mt 18:19–20).

Jesus was at prayer in the garden at Gethsemane (Mt 26:36–46), and in his Sermon on the Mount he gives us the model of prayer in the Our Father (Mt 6:10–13).

Jesus also is seen in the Gospels as a teacher. In his teaching he used a variety of the experiences of the people of the time to convey his message. Sometimes he taught in parables; at other times he offered commentaries on the Jewish Law. Probably most familiar to all of us are the stories of healings or miracles he performed. Miracles were not performed as proofs of Jesus' power but as signs of the coming of the kingdom of God. In whatever way Jesus selected to teach, we find the message to be the same: his mission was to prepare people for the coming of the kingdom.

Jesus suffered during his life because many misunderstood who he was and why he had come. Even his apostles misunderstood him and eventually deserted him—particularly at the time of his death. He was forced to endure the agony of the trial, the taunts of the mob following the trial, and the suffering on the cross. To understand the anguish and suffering of Jesus, one has only to read the story of Jesus in the garden of Gethsemane where he prays that the hour might pass (Mt 26:36–42) or to hear the words of Jesus on the cross: "My God, my God, why have you forsaken me?" (Mt 27:46). Yet in obedience to the Father we see that Jesus yielded up his spirit willingly to the Father. A man who lived obedient to the Father in life lived this total obedience even to the moment of death.

The Gospels do not end with Jesus' death but rather show that his death was only a passing phase. On the third day Jesus was raised from the dead by his heavenly Father to whom he willingly gave up his life. All four accounts of the Gospel give us the story of Jesus' resurrection from the dead (Mt 28; Mk 16; Lk 24: Jn 20).

A summation of the Gospel portrayal of Jesus of Nazareth would certainly include one who was faithful and obedient to his Father. We see clearly that Jesus came to proclaim that people were to repent (a radical conversion) because of the arrival of the reign of God. He was a man of deep prayer, a man who lived his life and freely shared it with others, who enjoyed deep and loving friendships. He suffered when people doubted him, demanded of him signs to prove himself, and even mocked and tried to humiliate him. Yet Jesus cared for all people, whether they were rich or poor, accepted or rejected by society. He was not afraid to speak out on the issues even when it was not wise or popular to do so. Even two thousand years after his life here on earth, his message is still relevant to us today. His message of care, love, and hope is a constant source of strength to each of us who has accepted him and believed.

This section only gives us a cursory, superficial view of the man named Jesus. These are simple thoughts gathered from virtually the only sources we have: the accounts of the Gospel according to Matthew, Mark, Luke, and John. A catechist should constantly be returning to the sources. Read the Gospels again and again. Reflect on them. Pray over them. Read Scripture commentaries. No one can ever exhaust one's knowledge of Jesus.

QUESTIONS FOR REFLECTION

1. What is your understanding of Jesus? _____
_____
_____
_____
_____

2. Using one of the Gospel accounts, substantiate your understanding. Indicate by chapter and verse. _____
_____
_____
_____
_____

3. If not all your ideas are found in that particular Gospel account, look for it in the other accounts. Indicate by chapter and verse. _____
_____
_____
_____
_____

4. If any of your ideas are not to be found in any of the Gospel accounts, ask yourself why.

_____
_____
_____
_____

2. THE APOSTLES' AND THE CHURCH'S GROWING UNDERSTANDING OF JESUS

A few years ago a docudrama was presented on television about the life of Martin Luther King. It was a very moving production, but what was of interest was how the image of Dr. King had grown in the decade after his death. While King was alive, his followers did not realize the significance of who he was and what he had done. Events like the Birmingham bus boycott, the Selma march, and the Memphis garbage workers' strike did not seem of historic moment as they happened. Their real significance only emerged in retrospect. The stature of Dr. King and his important place in history have emerged with hindsight. Historians of the 1980's will write about King with a different understanding than commentators of the 1950's and 1960's.

Something similar can be said of the life of Jesus. What we see in the Gospels is *not* the life of Jesus as his disciples actually saw it while he was alive, but rather the life of Jesus as his followers viewed him in retrospect a generation or more later. Events which seem so significant in the Gospels were not necessarily seen in the same light when Jesus was alive. Who Jesus is and why he came were discovered gradually through the reflections of the apostles and the other members of that community of believers which we refer to as the early Church. By examining the formation of the Gospels, we can come to an appreciation of how the apostles and the early Church grew in their understanding of who Jesus was.

There were very few people who witnessed the deeds and words of Jesus. Even his own followers did not realize fully who Jesus was. They saw him as their leader and teacher but very likely did not see him as the Messiah. The Twelve were willing to give up their occupations and sacrifice their lives to some degree to follow Jesus. However, their personal experience at that time was at best a very human one.

The death of Jesus seemed to add to the confusion. His followers were frightened; they were leaderless. As we know, Judas betrayed him, and Peter denied him. What seemed to be an ending became a beginning. With Jesus' death came the life of the Church. The event by which Jesus died, rose, and returned to the Father became the central event of Christianity. It is called the paschal mystery.

At some point these followers of Jesus were called to make a leap of faith: a faith that enabled them to see that Jesus was truly alive, truly risen, but in a different way. The event by which Jesus' followers, filled with the Holy Spirit, responded to the paschal mystery with a leap of faith is called "Pentecost." Luke describes the event in Acts 2.

> To appreciate the Pentecost event and the effect it had on Jesus' followers, you may want to read at this time Acts 2.

Following the Pentecost event, the vision of Jesus' followers changed. They began to review the life of Jesus in a different light. Events that seemed rather ordinary took on new meaning. They began to see a pattern to Jesus' life. There were messianic overtones. Jesus talked about the coming of the kingdom when he was alive, but now they realized that Jesus was the coming of the kingdom. The messianic prophecies had been fulfilled. Even the strange Isaian prophecies of the suffering servant (Isaiah 50—53) seemed to have been fulfilled in Jesus.

Once the followers or disciples of Jesus responded in faith and had a new vision, they also had this overwhelming urge to share that vision. Thus their immediate response to the Pentecost event was to proclaim what had happened. They went forth preaching the "good news," the Gospel. "Gospel" in its original sense refers to this preaching about Jesus and his message of salvation by his Spirit-filled followers in order to bring others to Jesus. The most accurate accounts of this original "Gospel" are found in the Acts of the Apostles. Here Luke recounts these sermons of the apostles.

> Acts 2:14–36 is the first of several apostolic sermons. You may want to read and reflect on this passage at this time.

During these early years of the Church, this apostolic preaching was a very fluid thing. There was no set script. The more the followers of Jesus preached and the more they reflected on the Christ-event, the more they came to know about Jesus and his message. This preaching about the good news is often referred to as the "kerygma," taken from a Greek word meaning "proclamation." As the preaching spread to various parts of the Roman empire, the kerygma began to vary a little according to where it was preached. For the first thirty to forty years there was no written Gospel as we see it today.

The written accounts of the Gospel according to Matthew, Mark, and Luke as we know it today were probably not written until around 70 A.D. These three accounts of the good news represent more developed reflections upon the Christ-event and a clearer understanding of who Jesus was. In each of those three accounts, there are slight variations from one another in emphasis and thematic development. This is natural. Although the original source was the same, each account is based upon a different kerygma: Matthew's on the apostolic preaching of the Church in Palestine, Mark's on that of the Church in Rome, and Luke's on that of the Church in Antioch. No single account is more "correct" than the others. Each views the same Christ-event from a different view. Taken together they gave the early Church an even clearer understanding of who Jesus was.

The Gospel according to John, written about a generation later than the other three, provides still another view. Being further removed than the other three from the time of Jesus, this account is probably not as exact a portrayal of the words and deeds of Jesus. But at the same time it reflects a clearer understanding of who Jesus is and a more mature reflection of the Christ-event. All four accounts are recognized by the Church as written under the inspiration of the Holy Spirit and hence a part of the Sacred Scriptures.

Some of the earliest and most beautiful reflections on the Christ-event are found in the writings of a man who never even saw Jesus of Nazareth in the flesh. Saul of Tarsus experienced his "Pentecost event" on the road to Damascus. It is related three times in Acts (9:1–9; 22:3–16; 26:2–18). After he put his faith in Christ, Saul took the name Paul and proceeded to preach with the same zeal and fervor as the original followers of Jesus. It is through Paul's writings that the Church sees herself as the living body of Christ. Largely through Paul's reflections, the early Church leaders, meeting in Jerusalem in 50 A.D., affirmed that mankind is saved through faith in Christ alone, not in the Mosaic law.

Although the last book of Scripture was completed, the quest for a deeper understanding of Jesus continued. Controversies arose among the early Christians and led to an even more developed understanding of Christ. Docetists denied that Christ was really a man while Arians denied that Christ was really God. Out of these controversies, the believing Church reflected and came forth with a clearer delineation of Jesus: one who is both human and divine. As divine, he is one of a Trinity: Father, Son, and Spirit. And reflections on Jesus continue.

Our own understanding of Jesus requires growth. When we were young children, our parents might have given us our first introduction to him. It was most likely a very human concept of Jesus—perhaps not that much different than Peter's first understanding of him. First Communion may have given us a different relationship with him as we realized that we were actually receiving him in our bodies. If our faith deepened, Jesus' love for us as well as his expectation of us may have become clearer. The greater our understanding of Jesus, the more he should seem a part of our life. Paul once said: "It is now no longer I that live, but Christ lives in me." Because Christ became such a part of his life, Paul's every action became Christ-centered and Christ-motivated. His missionary endeavors, his hardships and trials, grew out of that. Perhaps it is appropriate at this time to reflect on our own lives to examine our understanding of Jesus.

QUESTIONS FOR REFLECTION

1. Am I not seeking a greater understanding of Jesus?

2. Is not my very presence in this course a sign of this? _____
_____
_____
_____
_____

3. To what extent do my actions reflect my understanding of Jesus and the Christ-event? _____
_____
_____
_____
_____

4. What has been my "Pentecost event"? _____
_____
_____
_____
_____

3. THE INCARNATION: THE HUMANITY OF CHRIST

A number of movies and television programs are about people with amazing physical attributes. The six million dollar man and the bionic woman, reconstructed by the wonders of science, possess a strength and speed far beyond the capabilities of the rest of mankind. In the recent movie *Superman* the hero, a transplant from the planet Krypton, was able to save the state of California from sinking into the Pacific Ocean after an atomic bomb had created a massive earthquake.

Whether it is through ancient mythology or through these modern heroes of science fiction, all peoples have a tendency or need to produce their superstars. As Christians we tend to attribute such characteristics to Jesus. Yet despite the title of the rock opera, Jesus Christ was no superstar. He was no extraordinary creature from another planet. When John's Gospel says, "The Word became flesh" (Jn 1:14), it means that God did indeed became human. Jesus was truly one of us.

This section deals with the humanity of Christ for the very simple reason that Catholics have real difficulty accepting that humanity, although they have always accepted rather easily the fact that Christ was God. The Protestant tradition, on the other hand, has more difficulty accepting the divinity of Christ while more easily accepting his humanity. Historically, the docetist heresy, which denied Christ's humanity, preceded any heresy denying his divinity.

To accept in its fullest sense that Jesus was a human being means to understand what it is to be fully human. Although Jesus was not conceived through a human father, all growth and development took place in Jesus as it did in us. His abilities during those nine months before birth were as limited as ours were. He could not have survived without the nourishment of his mother. His organs developed only gradually. And he came forth into the world precisely as we were born—totally helpless. He had no more strength, no more ability for independent survival than we had as infants.

Jesus grew up as a Jew in that region of Palestine called Galilee in the village of Nazareth. Mary was his mother, and Joseph, a carpenter, was his father. Jesus spoke the only language he knew: Aramaic. As he grew up he learned as we did—experientially. His parents taught him to dress, eat, drink, and all the usual actions and activities any child learns. He learned about the Jewish Law from one of the local rabbis—probably a devotee of the liberal Hillel school of rabbinic thought.

In view of this it is appropriate to mention the incident of the finding of Jesus in the temple (Lk 2:41–52). When his parents were returning from their annual visit to the temple in Jerusalem, Jesus somehow was left behind.

> Not finding him, they returned to Jerusalem in search of him. On the third day they came upon him in the temple sitting in the midst of the teachers, listening to them and asking them questions. All who heard him were amazed at his intelligence and his answers (Lk 2:45–47).

Why their amazement? Did Jesus give answers that they had never heard before? No. Did his divine nature enable him to stump these scholars of the Law? No. They were amazed at how bright this boy was. He obviously studied hard the teachings of his rabbi. What most likely was really the surprise to them was that a Galilean should be so bright. They might expect a student from one of the Jerusalem academies to exhibit such erudition, but not a boy from the country. A person with such a thick Galilean accent was not ordinarily associated with this brilliance.

Like any human being Jesus experienced emotion. He was saddened at the death of the widow's son (Lk 7:13). He grew angry at the money changers in the temple (Mk 11:15–17). He was upset when his disciples tried to dismiss the children (Lk 18:15–16). He must have been amused when he saw the short man, Zacchaeus, climbing a sycamore tree to get a better look at him (Lk 19:1f). And he certainly experienced doubt and depression during his agony in the garden (Mt 26:36–46) and death on the cross.

Now let us look at the knowledge of Jesus. This is the area where people ordinarily find the greatest difficulty in understanding the relationship between the humanity and the divinity of Christ. If we said that Jesus was not able to fly, or could not move at the speed of sound, or could not see through buildings, few would have difficulty accepting that. But should we say that Jesus had limits to his knowledge, then suddenly people begin to feel that his divinity has been removed. Yet if Jesus was truly human, he did not know the future, did not speak

Greek or Latin, and could not read people's minds. Jesus' knowledge was acquired the same way as ours: through the senses.

Where the difficulty lies is in the very concept of "knowledge." God is so totally different from us that any analogy comparing his knowledge to ours breaks down. It is perhaps even confusing to use that same word for God and us. It would be like trying to use the word "travel" in reference to God.

Let us say that you are lost at sea and finally drift to some distant isle in the midst of the Pacific Ocean. The people there take you in. However, you do not know their language or understand their customs. Because of who you are you may know a lot of things: the English language, mathematics, the latest popular songs, television, automobiles, and washing machines. But all that knowledge is of no use for you right now in this culture. You need to learn all about the people's customs and language. Your knowledge is then extremely limited. Eventually you will be able to articulate in terms of these people who you are, but it must be articulated through the customs, thought patterns, and language of these people.

Jesus was in a similar situation. Because he emptied himself of his divinity to become one of us, he had to begin from scratch. He may have always "known" he was God but only in God's mode of knowledge. Since a baby is incapable of understanding or articulating so profound an idea as the nature of God, Jesus could not know fully in human terms who he was. Through the teachings of the rabbi Jesus began to learn about the Law and who God was. Jesus' knowledge did not come automatically. He had to study hard to learn the Law. As he grew up, his understanding of God became clearer. Out of this Jesus also developed a life of prayer. All the Gospel accounts tell us that Jesus spent long periods of time in communion with God. These periods drew him ever closer to his heavenly Father. Jesus gradually came to an awareness in human terms of who he was. He finally could articulate who he was because his human nature had developed to that point. It was because Jesus developed his humanity perfectly that he came to an awareness of his divinity. He came to know in human terms what he already knew in divine terms.

At no time did Jesus' limitations come out so clearly as in the final hours of his life. Jesus did not totally know what was to happen to him. In the garden of Gethsemane he said:

> "Abba (O Father), you have the power to do all things. Take this cup
> away from me. But let it be as you would have it, not as I" (Mk 14:36).

Despite his own doubts and hesitations, he was able to resign himself to the will of God because he lived his humanity perfectly. Perhaps his darkest moment came as he was dying on the cross at Calvary. Quoting the psalmist Jesus cried almost in desperation: "My God, my God, why have you forsaken me?" (Mk 15:34). Yet at the same time he could forgive the repentant thief (Lk 23:40–43), and he was able to say to God as he breathed his last: "Father, into your hands I commend my spirit" (Lk 23:46). Not knowing or understanding the resurrection, Jesus could resign himself totally to God. His knowledge about life after death was perhaps less than ours. We have what Jesus did not have to look back on: the resurrection of Jesus from the dead.

There are passages in the Gospel accounts that seem to indicate that Jesus had special foreknowledge. He seemed to have known ahead of time that he was going to be delivered up, put to death, and rise from the dead on the third day (Mk 9:10–11). He seems to have known ahead of time that the temple of Jerusalem would be destroyed by the Romans in 70 A.D. (Lk 21:5–24). However, Scripture scholars are generally in agreement that what appears to be a knowledge of the future is really the work of the evangelist. In recounting many events the evangelist puts words into the mouth of Jesus which Jesus himself never said. Rather than being a deception, it was a common literary practice at that time.

To accept Jesus as fully human should be for us an inspiration rather than an obstacle. Precisely because Jesus was so completely human, we are able to identify with him. His divinity did not make his life easier. He knew deprivation, doubt, suffering, and temptation. The only thing Jesus did not experience was sin. He lived his humanity perfectly without sin. To sin is not to be human; it is to be less than human. Jesus was so perfectly, sinlessly human that he was God.

By raising Jesus from the dead in glory, God has enabled us also to be raised from the dead. St. Augustine once said: "God became man, so that man might become God." In the offertory prayer at Mass we pray: "May we come to share in the divinity of Christ who humbled himself to share in our humanity." Christ who shared so fully our human nature has enabled us to share in his divine nature.

None of us are mythological titans. We aren't bionic persons or supermen or wonderwomen. We can't prevent earthquakes or "run faster than a speeding bullet." We are humans who must try to live out our humanity as perfectly as Christ. "You must be made perfect as your heavenly Father is perfect" (Mt 5:48). By doing so we share by adoption in the nature of God which Christ shares by natural descent. But we share in it nonetheless. Let us reflect on these words of the First Letter of John:

> See what love the Father has bestowed on us
> in letting us be called children of God!
> Yet that is what we are.
> The reason the world does not recognize us
> is that it never recognized the Son.
> Dearly beloved,
> we are God's children now;
> what we shall later be has not yet come to light.
> We know that when it comes to light
> we shall be like him,
> for we shall see him as he is (1 Jn 3:1–2).

QUESTIONS FOR REFLECTION

1. What do you find particularly inspirational about the humanness of Jesus?

2. Why are we able to accept Jesus' divinity so much more easily than his humanity?

3. Read Mk 14:34 ff. When have you experienced what Jesus did at Gethsemane?

4. If Jesus were only divine, what would our relationship be to God then?

4. THE INCARNATION: THE ROLE OF MARY

Recently in the newspaper there appeared an article about a woman in her early twenties who had been adopted as a baby but who now was searching for her natural parents. This woman spent thousands of dollars and traveled all over the United States and parts of Europe in her quest. Although her natural mother had died, in the end she met her natural father for the first time.

The ending was a happy one, but what was of interest was the quest itself. The woman was strongly motivated out of her desire for identity. Knowing her roots was important to her, for she felt she had to know precisely where she was situated in history and how she was a part of mankind.

One of the most profound phrases of Scripture is: "The Word became flesh and made his dwelling among us" (Jn 1:14). Suddenly God entered into our history. The implications are profound. How do we begin understanding what it means for God to become human?

Like the young woman our quest for Christ's identity as a human should begin by a search for his roots. In fact, two of the Gospels give us a genealogy of Jesus (Mt 1:1–7; Lk 3:23–38). Both infancy accounts (Mt 1:18–24; Lk 1:26–38) tell us that Mary conceived Jesus without a human father, and our Church tradition puts its belief in the virgin conception: "born of the Virgin Mary" (Apostles' Creed).

Luke 1:26–38 tells us that the angel Gabriel was sent by God to announce to Mary her role in salvation as the mother of the Messiah. Gabriel's greeting to Mary says much about how we ourselves see her:

> "Rejoice, O highly favored daughter! The Lord is with you. Blessed are you among women" (Lk 1:29).

Because of Mary's unique role in human history, we honor her above all others. It is Jesus alone who has redeemed us from sin and given us a share in God's life. But Jesus has redeemed us because God became human in the person of Jesus. It was because Mary was the one who brought Jesus into the world that the Word could become flesh. You and I are not needed for God's plan of salvation to take place. But Mary is.

> Mary said: "I am the servant of the Lord. Let it be done as you say" (Lk 1:38).

That "yes" enabled God to enter completely into human history as one of us.

When Mary consented to God's plan for her, she most likely had no idea that she was to be the mother of God. There is no assurance that even in Jesus' lifetime she knew fully who Jesus was. When Gabriel came, Mary was barely a teenager. But she was totally open to the will of God. Her life was that of complete receptivity to the action of God within her. She was highly favored by God, but Mary totally cooperated with God's favor. She alone was fit to bring the Word of God into our world because she alone was sinless. Her unique role in salvation meant that God filled her with his enduring presence from the moment of her conception. The Church has expressed this unique favor granted Mary by the term "immaculate conception" (not to be confused with "virgin birth" or "virgin conception"). In other words, Mary was conceived, as we were, by two parents, but from the first moment of her existence she was without original sin.

We have all been redeemed by the death and resurrection of Jesus Christ and share in the life of the Father. Mary was chosen to be the one human through whom Jesus Christ came into being. She who begot the God-man so that he might redeem us is herself most perfectly redeemed. Mary's redemption was a necessary part of God-become-human. Since Mary is human, and therefore free, her divine favor did not force her to love God. Although Christ, being God, could not sin, Mary could have sinned but did not. Her "yes" to God enabled

God to become one of us, but her "yes" then and throughout her life was nonetheless a free decision on her part.

An earlier reflection of the teaching Church than the immaculate conception was that Mary is the mother of God. At one time it was an extremely controversial statement. Yet it was a most important one, for on it hinged the identity of Christ. To speak of Mary as the mother of Jesus alone or of only the human nature of Christ is to distort the identity and mission of Christ. One is not a parent to a nature but to a person. The person Jesus was both human and divine. That he was both is the central element through which salvation has occurred. That God could exist in man is central to our faith. So the Church finally had to make it an official teaching that Mary indeed is the mother of God.

Mary is the person who links the era of Israel, the era of Christ, and the era of the Church. She was born a Jew and raised in accordance with the Law of Moses. She alone was present as the Word of God was conceived in her womb and the era of Christ began. She was present at Cana at the beginning of Jesus' public ministry (Jn 2:1–11). Mary was present at the foot of the cross as Jesus died (Jn 19:25). Then with the resurrection of Christ comes the era of the Church. Mary was very much a part of the life of the early Church (Acts 1:14).

Have you experienced a certain peace amid turmoil because a certain person was near? Very often we might appreciate someone not because he or she did something for us but because that person was present to us. There are some individuals who can affect the conversation of a group or an individual because they are present. This perhaps may be a way of describing the role of Mary. Her presence was effective.

We saw that at all the critical events of salvation history Mary was present. But she also became to others a presence of the Holy Spirit. In her earthly life Mary did not do much in human terms. But because she was filled with the Holy Spirit her very presence affected the lives of others. She enabled the Holy Spirit to touch them. It was that presence that enabled Joseph to accept Mary as his wife though she was pregnant by another (Mt 1:20–21). Mary's presence enabled Elizabeth joyfully to praise Mary as Elizabeth felt the baby in her womb leap for joy (Lk 1:41–45). That presence of Mary drew the shepherds (Lk 2:16) and the magi (Mt 2:11) to the Messiah. Because of who she was, Mary was able to draw out the best in others and lead them closer to God. That same presence must have had a profound effect on the life and growth of the early Church.

When Jesus was dying on the cross we find Jesus turning to his mother Mary to speak to her of her important role in salvation:

> Seeing his mother there with the disciple whom he loved, Jesus said to his mother, "Woman, there is your son." In turn he said to the disciple, "There is your mother." From that hour onward, the disciple took her into his care (Jn 19:26–27).

The Church has seen these words as commissioning Mary as mother of the Church. She who was the first redeemed stands as the perfect model of all of us who are a part of that community of the redeemed that we call the Church.

The fathers of Vatican II called Mary the archetype of the Church. What God asked of Mary he also asks of us. What God does to Mary he also does to us. What Mary does in response to God we also are to do. If we begin to interchange Mary and Church, we will understand more clearly how Mary is the perfect model or archetype of Church.

God has called Mary (Church) to bring Christ to the world. Mary (Church) responds with the words: "Let it be done to me as you say" (Lk 1:38). It is only through the free action of Mary (Church) that Christ is present in and to the world. It was through the action of the Holy Spirit in Mary (Church) that others perceived the presence of Christ and rejoiced at it (Lk 1:41–45). Mary (Church) in response is able to praise the presence of God to the world in the Magnificat. Read this prayer and place yourself in the position of Mary. As part of the Church you really are in that position.

> My being proclaims the greatness of the Lord,
>   my spirit finds joy in God my savior.
> For he has looked upon his servant in her lowliness;
>   all ages to come shall call me blessed.
> God who is mighty has done great things for me;
>   holy is his name.
> His mercy is from age to age
>   on those who fear him.
> He has shown might with his arm;
>   he has confused the proud in their inmost thoughts.
> He has deposed the mighty from their thrones
>   and raised the lowly to high places.
> The hungry he has given every good thing,
>   while the rich he has sent empty away.
> He has upheld Israel his servant,
>   ever mindful of his mercy,
> Even as he promised our fathers,
>   promised Abraham and his descendants forever (Lk 1:46–55).

As the perfect model of Church, Mary has already accomplished perfection which the Church someday will attain. She is therefore our inspiration and our hope. What may seem out of reach is attainable. We know this because Mary, one of our own, has herself already done it. Vatican II's *Constitution on the Church* says:

> But while in the Most Blessed Virgin the Church has already reached that perfection whereby it exists without spot or wrinkle (cf. Eph 5:27), the faithful still strive to conquer sin and increase in holiness. And so they turn their eyes to Mary who shines forth to the whole community of the elect as the model of virtues.... Seeking after the glory of Christ, the Church becomes more like its lofty type, and continually progresses in faith, hope and charity, seeking and doing the will of God in all

things. The Church, therefore, in its apostolic work too, rightly looks to her who gave birth to Christ, who was thus conceived of the Holy Spirit and born of a virgin, in order that through the Church he could be born and increase in the hearts of the faithful. In her life the Virgin has been a model of that motherly love with which all who join in the Church's apostolic mission for the regeneration of mankind should be animated (n. 65).

The crowning glory of Christ's life was his resurrection from the dead and return to the Father. This event, which we call the paschal mystery, is more than merely Christ's cashing in on his round-trip ticket. Christ as human rose from the dead in glory to share the life of the Father, so that we might do so also. Since Mary is our model and since she is intimately involved in Christ's mission of salvation, she is part of that resurrection. We saw in the immaculate conception that Mary anticipated the saving grace of Christ. Our resurrection from the dead is also anticipated in Mary according to the Church's teaching on the assumption of Mary. At the end of her life Mary rose ("was assumed"), body and soul, into heaven. Even in her death Mary stands as the perfect model of the Church. Mary shares fully, body and soul, in the glorified life of heaven. What Mary does to perfection, the Church likewise will do on the last day.

In light of this, our devotion to Mary is closely linked to our life as Christians. Our generation's growing sensitivity to the issues of social justice reflects a greater concern for our fellow human beings. Mary has already been doing that for each of us. As the most perfect Christian, Mary was and is constantly striving with the help of the Spirit to bring Christ to others and others to Christ. Her care is for even the most neglected. Maintaining a devotion to Mary must of necessity link us to a devotion to those same sisters and brothers of ours whom Mary cares for so much.

Our attitude toward Mary must avoid two extremes. If we put Mary apart from the Church of today, she becomes just another person who happened to bring the Messiah into the world a long time ago. If we put Mary apart from Church as someone above it, we make Mary into an idol. But as long as our love for Mary is related to the Church as its model and mother, Mary will enable us to draw out of the Church that which is tainted and see the good and the beauty of the Church and its potential for perfection.

QUESTIONS FOR REFLECTION

1. What person has had a profound effect on your life because of his or her presence? _____
_____
_____
_____
_____

2. In your life how has devotion to Mary brought you closer to Christ?_____
_____
_____
_____
_____

3. Mary said "yes" to God at the annunciation, not knowing what it would lead to but trusting in the Lord's word. Think of moments in your life where a deep faith in someone enabled you to take a step into the unknown and attain something you did not even imagine._____
_____
_____
_____
_____

4. The Second Vatican Council has called Mary model of the Church. How do you personally view Mary as this model? What events in her life particularly exemplify this to you?_____
_____
_____
_____
_____

5. JESUS CHRIST THE SACRAMENT OF GOD

An article appeared in a Los Angeles newspaper about a young man committed to the Catholic Worker Movement on skid row. Finding Catholicism irrelevant to his life and concerns, he left the Church in his early college years and became actively involved in the anti-war movement in the late 1960's. His activism eventually led him to embrace a philosophy of radical Marxism. All of his efforts were directed toward the overthrow of the existing establishment.

One day while roaming aimlessly through skid row, he happened to saunter into the Catholic Worker center. There he encountered others who had many of the same concerns: commitment to the poor, pacifism, concern for prisoners, disdain for the hypocrisy of society. Since then he has devoted all his time and energy to serving the needs of others. His commitment to the cause was so strong that he was arrested for trying to procure cast-off food for the poor from the trash bins of the Farmer's Market, for a tax protest outside the Federal Building, and for an anti-nuclear weapons protest. He has freely chosen to live among the poor and has renounced all possessions.

Who is this person? The name does not matter. His deeds say much more about who he is than his name or the words which he says. His actions are for us the sign by which we are able to encounter the person. In fact, they are really the way in which we can come to know this person or any person.

> Jesus did not accept the arbitrary standards of his day. He sought no place of power; he refused kingship; he bought no home; he praised mercy over sacrifice, need over the suffocation of wealth; he preferred the lilies of the field to political favor. Jesus lived life. He was no slave to the conventional values of either a Judaic or a Roman system.
>
> Jesus lived life. He gave himself to those who needed him rather than to those who had all they needed. He was concerned with a few loaves and fishes, with prophecy and Fatherhood, faith and flowers. He cared for these realities because he sought to reveal life's deepest meaning. We can dismiss his message but we should not do this while we call ourselves Christians unless, of course, we are not troubled by our own hypocrisy. (Anthony Padovano, *Dawn Without Darkness,* Paulist Press, pp 16–18)

In this unit and in our reading of the Scriptures we have seen the events and the actions of Jesus. It was through the Church's reflections on the events and actions of Jesus that it came to a realization that Jesus was more than just a man: he also was God. Through the events and actions of Jesus we come to encounter the person of Jesus. Since that same person Jesus was also God, the events and actions of Jesus were in reality the events and actions of God. The signs by which we encountered Jesus are the signs by which we encounter God. A sacrament is a living sign by which we encounter a person. Jesus can then be called the sacrament of God. Jesus is the most perfect way of coming to know who God is. He is the living, breathing, walking, talking sign to the world of who God is. God, who is totally other, totally distant, totally transcendent, becomes present and immanent in the person of Jesus.

QUESTIONS FOR REFLECTION

1. What are the signs by which people know us?

2. What are the actions that would speak about who we are?

3. Describe what actions of yours speak clearly about who you are. _____
_____
_____
_____
_____

Unit Three

COMMUNITY OF FAITH

1. FORMATION OF COMMUNITY AS PEOPLE OF FAITH

A tragic occurrence of our day has been the plight of the Vietnamese "boat people." Unwilling to live any longer under the oppressive tyranny of their mother country, thousands have fled by boat over strange waters in search of a country that would accept them. Most of the people perished at sea. Countries were unwilling to admit them. Yet the "boat people" pushed on persistently.

Some finally did find a country which would accept them. They settled down, eventually found work, and became productive members of the new society. Yet among themselves they had developed a strong feeling of solidarity. They stuck together. They supported one another. They shared a common experience and retained common memories. This provided a common bond for their community. Because of their strong bond of community, these former "boat people" became a source of strength and support for one another.

There was another group of people who also shared a common experience: the disciples of Jesus. Their common bond was their faith in Jesus. They believed that Jesus was sent by God into the world to save us. "This is the Jesus God has raised up, and we are his witnesses" (Acts 2:32). The resurrection of Jesus from the dead is the basis of their faith. Luke describes the first movement of faith for the followers of Jesus on the day of Pentecost.

Read Acts 2:1–12

Although the experience of these followers of Jesus was not a tragic one like that of the "boat people," it was a common experience that provided the basis for their solidarity. The faith-filled followers had an ineluctable urge to tell others about it. They also felt a need to preserve that common experience by coming together to form a community. This community not only was formed; it grew. Three thousand people were baptized on Pentecost alone. Acts describes the life of this early community:

> They devoted themselves to the apostles' instruction and the communal life, to the breaking of bread and the prayers. A reverent fear overtook them all, for many wonders and signs were performed by the apostles. Those who believed shared all things in common; they would sell their property and goods, dividing everything on the basis of each one's need. They went to the temple area together every day, while in their homes they broke bread. With exultant and sincere hearts they took their meals in common, praising God and winning the approval of all the people. Day by day the Lord added to their number those who were being saved (Acts 2:42–47).

Even in the time immediately following the resurrection of Jesus we have the essential elements of Church. As the number of believers grew, the Church became more highly structured. There were bishops, priests, and deacons. A hierarchy became more monarchical. Yet the need for community was still an essential element. People need to share their faith experience, learn from one another about Christ, minister to one another, and support one another. Once the sense of community is lost, Church becomes a sterile, almost empty concept.

Ask children what they think of when you say "Church." Many will say: "It's the place where I have to go on Sunday." Or they might say: "The priests and sisters." Ask most adults what they think of when you say "Church." They might say "the Pope and bishops" or "the teaching authority." It is not very often that they will see Church as "the community of believers." The problem is not necessarily with them. It's simply that they have never had a real experience of community connected with their Church. There has been poor catechesis on the community aspect of Church because there has not been enough experience of community formation. "To Teach as Jesus Did," the pastoral letter of the bishops of the United States, says:

> Community is at the heart of Christian education not simply as a concept to be taught but as a reality to be lived. Through education, men must be moved to build community in all areas of life; they can do this best if they have learned the meaning of community by experiencing it (n. 23).

A built-in obstacle to a sense of community is the sheer size of some of our parishes. How does one have a sense of community in a parish of two, three, four, or five thousand families when it seems as if you never see the same person twice? Or how does one have this sense of family in a church full of worshipers whom you don't even know? Even in such a large group, community does exist. The worshipers may not know one another, but they do know that they are drawn together to worship because of a common set of beliefs and values. To enable people to understand Church as a *community,* the Church must create situations that will enable people to experience community in a more intimate setting so that they will in turn realize that Church is also community in the large setting of Sunday liturgy.

As catechists we have the responsibility of helping to form community within our group of learners. It is an ideal setting for experiencing Church. The group is small. There is a common faith to share. There are a number of common experiences to share. There is a singleness of purpose. Catechists cannot create community automatically, but they can allow an atmosphere to exist so that community can happen. If there is an atmosphere of warmth, an attitude of respect for the learners, and a flexibility in the learning situation, community can happen. If all are made to feel that their feelings are important, community can occur.

QUESTIONS FOR REFLECTION

1. What has been your personal experience of community?_____
_____
_____
_____
_____

2. Have you experienced community with your fellow learners in this course? Describe._____
_____
_____
_____
_____

3. How would you help foster community as a catechist?_____
_____
_____
_____
_____

2. CHURCH AS PEOPLE OF GOD

The Second Vatican Council brought a totally different dimension from recent Church teaching when it described the Church as "the people of God." That concept included not just the Pope and bishops, not just the official teaching authority, not even just Roman Catholics, but the entire Christian community (see *Constitution of the Church,* n. 14).

This was really not a radically new vision of Church. It was solidly grounded in the Scriptures. The Israelite community saw themselves in these very terms. "I will be their God, and they shall be my people" (Jer. 31:33; Ez. 37:27). The First Letter of Peter was a baptismal homily addressed to the newly baptized:

> You, however, are "a chosen race, a royal priesthood, a holy nation, a people he claims for his own to proclaim the glorious works" of the One who called you from darkness into his marvelous light. Once you were no people, but now you are God's people (1 Pt. 2:9–10).

To describe the Church as the people of God is as traditional as one can get.

Yet is that how most people see themselves? That most certainly has not been the model of Church that we grew up with. Our life in the Church prior to Vatican II was lived very much within our individual life of prayer. Any signs of communal participation were at best minimal. We gathered because of our oneness in belief but in reality more out of a sense of obligation. We listened in a language that was not our own to a priest whose face was not seen because he faced the altar rather than the congregation. Our missals had pictures of the posture of the priest, and most often this was our map: it offered the starting point, distinctions in between, and finally the conclusion. We were there to observe in silence or say our own personal prayers privately.

If people were to ask what religion we professed, we would have answered, of course: "Catholic." Were they to ask further how we participated, few would have even known what "participation" meant. Often during Mass some prayed the rosary, others used their missals, while still others made a novena to the Blessed Mother or a favorite saint. Our "participation" in church was very much tied to our own thing. The many rituals that took place were never clearly understood by most people. In fact, upon departing from Mass it was rare to hear anyone discuss what had taken place. The people did not feel a part of the Mass or a part of the life of the Church. Participation was not their role. That was the role of priests and sisters. The priests were responsible for the sacramental life and the sisters for the educational life. The laity was on the receiving end except when it came to supporting the Church financially.

Somewhere between the First Letter of Peter and the Second Vatican Council, the scriptural image of Church as the people of God was lost. In the early centuries of the Church, Christians saw the Church in terms of the people of God. This people did not own large blocks of property. The Church was little more than a movement, a movement that often aroused the ire of, first, the Jewish leaders and, later, the Roman emperor.

Then an ominous event occurred in the fourth century. Emperor Constantine embraced the Christian religion. Although he himself was not actually baptized until on his deathbed, he did want all of his subjects to become Christians. Subsequent emperors followed suit, so that the state religion changed its allegiance from polytheism to Christianity. Until this time the Church was something one entered after a conversion experience and careful preparation. Now everyone was to be baptized, and the sooner the better. Even infants were baptized. To be a Christian was like being a citizen: it just happened to you. The era of Christendom had begun.

The fifth through ninth centuries brought on the barbarian invasion. Almost all religious literature was preserved in monasteries, particularly by the Irish monks. But much of the tradition of the Church was never assimilated by anyone else. The Church eventually assimilated the barbarians into its midst but with no catechetical preparation. There were mass baptisms. To become a Christian involved no real conversion. It was done for you. The Church was seen by people in relation to those who baptized them. The Church made them Christians, but they did not see themselves as Church. Since the barbarians did not even speak the language of the Empire, Latin, the language in which the Church worshiped was foreign to them.

From the time of Constantine, passing through the Dark Ages and medieval times, the Church became more closely allied to the state. Bishops became feudal lords, and the Church owned vast tracts of property. People saw themselves as obeying their bishops much as they obeyed their lords or barons. They had as much responsibility with what went on in the Church as they did with what went on in their lord's fiefdom.

The Renaissance brought on new ideas and new structures of government. Nations began to be formed out of feudal states. This era also brought on the Protestant Reformation. The Church was on the defensive. National sovereignty was a threat to its secular power, and the Protestant Reformation was a threat to its religious power. The Church hierarchy became, if anything, more defensive and more protective of what it had to say regarding Church affairs. The hierarchy was too concerned with preserving the status quo to broaden the participation of Church members.

The revolutions of the eighteenth and nineteenth centuries brought on a greater involvement of the people in the affairs of government. Kings lost their absolute power, and democracy was on the rise. But the Church was still clinging to its feudal power. In fact, until the middle of the nineteenth century, the Pope himself was still a feudal lord ruling the Vatican States in various parts of Italy. Pope Pius IX bitterly fought any attempts to unify Italy as a nation, for that would mean relinquishing his temporal sovereignty.

As long as the Pope himself was a temporal monarch, it would be difficult to change the image of Church from a monarchical structure. The First Vatican Council (1869–70) came up with its own *Constitution on the Church*. However, due to the Franco-Prussian War, the document was only partially completed.

One of the chapters that was completed and promulgated was the dogma on papal infallibility. Declaring that the Pope when speaking solemnly ("ex cathedra") on matters of faith and morals speaks without fear of error, the dogma only further intensified the image of the Church as a monarchical structure. Even the bishops were left out of it.

With the loss of the papal states, the Pope no longer needed to be concerned about being a temporal monarch. It wasn't, however, until 1929 that a pope fully accepted the loss of his temporal power. That year Pope Pius XI signed the Lateran Pact with Mussolini, thereby officially accepting Italy as a nation.

Another phenomenon was occurring along with the loss of the Church's temporal power: the emergence of the Catholic laity. Because of a growing literacy rate throughout the Christian world, the priest was no longer the only educated or even the most educated person in the parish. People no longer were as readily inclined to accept the priest as the absolute authority on everything. As the people had a greater participation over civil affairs, it was only natural that they would come to a greater participation in Church affairs.

The signs of the times moved the bishops of Vatican II to rethink their model of Church. In rethinking the model, they found that they did not need to create something totally new. Rather they went back to their own tradition, a tradition grounded in the Old Testament and continued in the Church by Peter himself: the Church as the "people of God."

The "people of God," therefore, are those called by the Father. They are called to share in the prophetic office of Christ. We are not to be passive onlookers, but rather a people of the Word, responsible for proclaiming it to others and living it out in our lives by utilizing the various gifts that we have received.

QUESTIONS FOR REFLECTION

1. Seeing this brief historical survey, why do you think we veered away from that biblical notion of Church as people of God?

2. What are the identifiable marks in your journey by which others would see you as part of the people of God?

3. Read an issue of the *National Catholic Reporter* and the *National Catholic Register*. Each represents a different viewpoint of Church. How does each contribute as part of the people of God? _____
_____
_____
_____
_____

4. Looking back over the last 20 years, what have been your different images of Church? _____
_____
_____
_____
_____

3. CHURCH AS SACRAMENT OF CHRIST

One of the more famous attractions of Moscow is the tomb of Lenin. Millions of Soviet citizens and curious foreigners file past his body to gaze at the father of bolshevism. The wonders of modern science have enabled his body to be preserved from corruption so that he looks virtually the same as the day he died. It would seem to be the way in which the Soviets can keep the memory and the spirit, if not the person, of Lenin alive.

A science fiction movie entitled *The Boys from Brazil* treated the subject of human cloning. A mad Nazi scientist took tissue samples from the body of Adolf Hitler before he died and preserved them for a number of years. When this scientist had perfected the technique of human cloning, he was able to produce carbon copies of Hitler. His master plan was that with a group of Hitlers the Third Reich could rise again and conquer the world.

In both cases we have an attempt to prolong the life of a charismatic leader and founder of a movement in order to keep that movement alive. Jesus came to announce the coming of the kingdom. But that kingdom was not established fully in Jesus' lifetime. Its establishment was to be a gradual process of generations. Yet Jesus Christ was to be the way by which the kingdom was to come. Somehow in order to link the time of Christ to the time when the kingdom was to be fully established, there had to be some kind of "cloning process," some means of keeping Christ alive even after he died. The key to this missing link is an event which we call the paschal mystery.

By paschal mystery we mean that event by which Christ, having died, was raised by the power of the Father, and is truly risen and alive among us. Christ's earthly existence had its limitations. He was confined to time and space. But the paschal mystery gave Christ a new existence. His glorified body could make him present in a myriad of ways. He could be present to each and every one of us without limits. An encounter with Christ becomes a reality for all ages.

We called Jesus the sacrament of God since he was the visible, living sign of God. There is likewise a sacrament by which we encounter Jesus. Since a sacrament is a living sign by which we encounter a person, the Church can be called the sacrament of Christ. It is the visible extension of Jesus in the world today. As Vatican II says:

> All those who in faith look toward Jesus, the author of salvation and the principle of unity and peace, God has gathered together and established as the Church, that it may be for each and every one the visible sacrament of this saving unity (*Constitution on the Church,* n. 9).

The mystery of our faith is that Christ is risen and living through his believers. *We* are the living presence of Christ in the world. St. Paul says that we are the body of Christ (1 Cor. 12:12–27). Christ does not remain alive through cloning or deep freeze techniques. He remains alive through the community of believers who are united together as a body under Christ their head, striving to establish fully the kingdom on earth.

To call the Church a mystery or a sacrament is to say the same thing. Both words imply an external, visible element beneath which lies a deeper, invisible reality. Ninety percent of an iceberg is beneath the water. The visible part, however, tells us of the invisible part below. What is visible in the Church also points to us what is invisible beneath the surface. To understand the complex mystery of the Church, it is helpful to review the formation of Church.

We begin with the experience of Jesus. While he was alive, that experience was confined to a very few. Before his resurrection, it was a very human experience—no more. It was no different than our encounters with our friends each day. But then came Jesus' resurrection from the dead on Easter Sunday and the challenge to his followers to respond in faith. Those who made that response of faith on Pentecost Sunday (Acts 2:1–13) suddenly had a new vision. Their experience of Jesus was illumined by the response of faith, a special gift of the Holy Spirit. Jesus' followers understood the meaning of Jesus' deeds and words much more deeply than they had when he was alive. They began to understand his identity as Messiah and his messianic mission.

Out of that new faith experience arose a strong desire to share it with others, as shown in Acts 2:14–40, for example. This is what we call "proclaiming the good news," or "preaching the Gospel," or "evangelizing." Sharing leads naturally to celebrating, so these faith-filled believers came together in prayer and relived these wonderful events in a public celebration which they called "the breaking of bread" (Acts 2:42) and we call the Eucharist. It was this sharing and praying together that gave this people a sense of community.

As the numbers of the followers of Jesus increased, they naturally needed to become more organized. The apostles were the selected leaders of the community because, chosen by Jesus while he was alive and preaching his message of salvation, they were the ones to bring the message of Jesus to others. Peter was to be the head of the Church (Mt. 16:18-19). Acts shows how an established hierarchy arose. A study of Church history could show us how the organization of the Church evolved to its present structure.

So all of these elements make up the mystery which we call Church: experience of Jesus, faith response, sharing, celebrating, organization. To concentrate on organization only is like accepting the tip of the iceberg. To reject the visible element of Church in order to encounter Christ directly is to deny the only way in which Christ is able to live today. Church is all these elements together as a single whole. It is when we live in full communion with all of these that we will really encounter the living reality of Jesus Christ.

To call the Church a sacrament means also keeping in mind how Church was described in the last section: people of God. We then are the sacrament of Christ. Christ was the living sign of God to the world. We are the living, breathing, walking, talking sign of Christ to the world. People will not find Christ through our Church if all they see in Church is a hierarchy, a building, or a teaching magisterium. It is not "real presence," "hypostatic union," "papal infallibility," or even "collegiality" that will bring people to the Church. It will be because they have encountered in us the living Christ, because we have been true signs of the reality we represent.

QUESTIONS FOR REFLECTION

1. Examine those five elements comprising the mystery of Church. Are each of those a part of your formation as a Christian? Which elements seem to predominate more than others?

2. How have you viewed Church as the sacrament of Christ? To what extent have you been a living sign of Christ to the world?

4. LITURGY: PUBLIC CELEBRATION OF THE FAITH COMMUNITY

A recent newspaper article told about a high school class that has been meeting annually since 1929. The people come from a variety of professions and walks of life. Among the group is the owner of a supermarket chain, a few doctors, several lawyers, salespersons, laborers, and a number of housewives. Some of them by now have retired. Although most of them still live locally, there are a few who travel across the country to attend this annual affair.

What is it that impels these people to come together so faithfully over the years? For them their high school years were very special ones. They had wonderful experiences together. They built up a certain sense of solidarity with one another because of these common experiences. They come together to celebrate their solidarity with one another and relive their common experience.

Let's walk inside the school auditorium and see what's happening. The main gathering place seems to be the bar. Food in one hand and a cocktail in the other seem to be part of the affair. As we listen in on the conversation, it's usually peppered with such phrases as: "Whatever happened to . . . ?" or "Remember the time when . . . ?" There is a feeling of good will, joy, and even laughter as many recount the pranks, the exams, the prom, and the different characters in the class. There might even be a touch of nostalgia as they recall graduation day.

It is obvious that this celebration, as enjoyable as it is, is not the most important event of the year. However, it is the peak experience each year for them as alumni of their school. They may run into their fellow graduates on a number of occasions during the year, but at no other time is their identity as alumni so expressive and so meaningful as during this celebration. In recalling their high school experience each year, they almost seem to relive that experience again and again. That is probably what really makes this annual reunion a celebration.

If any of you have ever attended a class reunion, if any of you have ever enjoyed sharing common experiences of the past, if you know the feeling of recalling and reliving these events, if you know what it is to celebrate with a group with whom you once grew up and studied, then you have a good idea of what it is to experience liturgy. Liturgy is the public action of the Christian faith community in which the saving event of Jesus Christ is recalled, relived, and celebrated.

Our liturgical celebration is much like a class reunion. The people meet regularly at the same place. They come from a variety of backgrounds and walks of life. Some people come from a great distance, although most come from the local area. They come to share a common experience: the paschal mystery. Although we ourselves were not physically present in Palestine when Jesus died and rose from the dead, it is part of our faith that when we were initiated into the Church through baptism we shared in the death and resurrection of Christ (Rom 6:3–13). Because we share this common experience we have a sense of solidarity with one another. Our active participation through conversation and singing makes us a part of the liturgical celebration.

This liturgy can hardly be called the most important event of our life. But our weekly celebration of liturgy does mark our peak moment as Christians. We may encounter our fellow Christians outside the liturgy but nowhere are we so much a faith community as when we celebrate the liturgy. The *Constitution on the Sacred Liturgy* says:

> The liturgy is the summit toward which the activity of the Church is directed; it is also the font from which all its power flows. For the goal of apostolic endeavor is that all who are made sons of God by faith and baptism should come together to praise God in the midst of his Church, to take part in the sacrifice and to eat the Lord's supper (n. 10).

Although the term liturgy usually means for us the Mass, the two terms are not completely interchangeable. Every one of the sacraments being administered is a liturgical action. In calling for the liturgical reform of the sacraments, the Second Vatican Council set forth these four principles:

1. Liturgy is an action of the whole body of the Church; it is not a private function (n. 26).
2. There must always be a proclamation of the word of God (n. 24).
3. The rite must be perceptible to the senses, for each is the nature of liturgy (n. 7).
4. It must be of such sort that the people as a community can participate in it (n. 14).

Although these principles apply to the reform of all the sacraments, at this time our attention will be directed to the liturgy of the Mass. The reform of the other sacraments will be taken up later.

1. *Liturgy is an action of the entire body of the Church; it is not a private function.* At one time if someone asked us who celebrated the liturgy, we would say the priest, period. Now we would answer that we all do. Various liturgical ministries are now shared in the celebration of the Mass. The priest presides, but other ministers include the lector, commentator, cantor, choir, ushers, acolytes, eucharistic ministers, and bearers of the gifts. When Jesus Christ is offered up on the altar, it is the whole body of Christ, head and members.

2. *There must be a proclamation of the Word of God.* To proclaim the Word of God is to call people to conversion. To enable the people to be exposed more extensively to the richness of the Scriptures, the reformed liturgy of Sunday has expanded the readings to include one from the Old Testament in addition to the epistle and Gospel. The readings also are on a three-year cycle rather than an annual one. The readings are to be followed by a homily, which is a reflection on the Word of God and how it speaks to Christians in their everyday life. If the

Word of God were merely read, it would simply be a look into the past. But because the Word of God is part of a liturgical celebration, it makes present, actualizes, the event which is lived today, by which Christ speaks his message to us and for us at that moment. The Word of God is not merely proclaimed; it is also acclaimed, meditated upon, commented on, accepted, and implored.

3. *The rite must be perceptible to the senses, for such is the nature of liturgy.* The language was changed from Latin to the vernacular so that what was heard could be understood. The prayers pertaining to the people were to be said by the celebrant audibly rather than silently. The altar was to be situated such so that the priest could celebrate the Eucharist facing the people; thus the people could observe easily the actions which the priest was performing. Symbols and symbolic actions which had lost meaning were done away with, and words often accompanied the gestures and symbolic actions to better clarify what actions were taking place.

4. *It must be such that the people as a community can participate in it.* Parts of the Mass formerly said by the server or priest alone are now shared with the people. The sung Mass is to be the norm with primarily congregational singing rather than choir singing. A dialogue between priest and people takes place in different places throughout the Mass.

Since Christ is present through the Word and through the Eucharist, the Mass involves two aspects: the liturgy of the Word and the liturgy of the Eucharist. When we come together to hear God's Word, we become disposed for the action of the paschal mystery. The Word of God calls us together, speaks with us and invites us in faith as the people of God in order to prepare us to offer ourselves with Christ to the Father on the altar of sacrifice. We celebrate the Word of God: proclamation (the three Scripture readings), meditation (periods of silence following each reading along with the responsorial psalm), acclamation (alleluia), commentary (homily), profession (creed), supplication (general intercessions or prayer of the faithful). We celebrate the Eucharist: preparation of the gifts (bread and wine), offering of Christ (calling to mind and making present the paschal mystery through the changing of bread and wine into the body and blood of Christ), and Communion (eating the body and blood of Christ).

Although members of the class of 1929 may many times recall their high school days when they are sitting at home, it is only when they come together as a group in their annual reunion that they are really able to relive that experience fully because they are able to express past events with others who have also lived it out. Although we may many times meditate on the saving events of our faith, it is only when we come together as a worshiping community that we are really able to relive that experience fully. As catechists we must not merely teach the facts of liturgy. We must bring people to an appreciation of the experience of liturgy. It is only then that our people can have a true liturgical sense.

LITURGICAL COLORS

GREEN — A sign of hope. This color is used at all Masses throughout the year when no special Mass or feast is celebrated. As Christians we are confidently hoping for the coming of Christ.

WHITE — A sign of joy. This color is used at all solemnities (Easter, Christmas, etc.), feasts and Masses of the Blessed Virgin, feasts and memorials of saints who are not martyrs, weddings, funerals, baptisms, devotions, and other Masses for special occasions.

VIOLET — A sign of penance. It is used for Masses during Advent and Lent and for either individual or communal celebrations of the sacrament of penance.

RED — A sign of blood or fire. It is used for feasts and memorials of martyrs who shed their blood for the faith. It is also used on Pentecost Sunday, at the sacrament of confirmation, and at Masses of the Holy Spirit as a reminder of the tongues of fire which indicated the coming of the Holy Spirit on the apostles on the first Pentecost.

LITURGICAL VESTMENTS

ALB — The full-length, white garment worn by the priest and deacon at all liturgical celebrations. *Alba* in Latin means "white."

CINCTURE — A rope wrapped around the waist to hold the alb in place. It is optional.

STOLE — A strip of cloth six to fifteen inches wide. It wraps around the back of the neck and hangs from both shoulders down below the knees. The stole is in the liturgical color of the day. It is worn by the priest whenever he is administering a sacrament. The stole of the deacon hangs from one shoulder across to the other side of the body.

CHASUBLE — The outer garment—like a cloak. It is in the color of the day and is worn by the celebrant only for Mass. Some vestments are designed for the stole to be worn over the chasuble rather than under it.

QUESTIONS FOR REFLECTION

1. What are the obstacles in your life that have created difficulties in your ability to celebrate?

2. How can we make our involvement at Sunday liturgy more meaningful?

3. How can ritual in liturgy nourish your faith life?

4. What events in your faith life have been celebrated through liturgy?

Unit Four

INITIATION INTO THE COMMUNITY OF FAITH

1. THE SACRAMENTS OF INITIATION

The United States of America has integrated myriads of different peoples within its borders. A variety of peoples have sought refuge in this land throughout its history. Even at this time our country is taking in many people from throughout the world. The reasons for coming are almost as many as the people. Koreans during and after the Korean conflict came in large numbers. Mexicans seeking an opportunity to find employment and a better standard of living arrive daily. Cubans and Vietnamese, fleeing from an oppressive state, have sought and been granted asylum.

The United States is now and always has been a mixture of people. They each have brought their traditions, cultures, and gifts to a country that has opened its doors and welcomed them. America has been greatly enriched by those who have arrived at their new home over the centuries.

Once settled in their "new home," many find they want to remain. They work, set up houses, seek education for their families, and build a sense of security. They have their identity and are guaranteed the right to maintain that identity.

These people may eventually become citizens of the country. This citizenship allows them certain rights and carries with it certain responsibilities. Some of these include the right to elect the officials who make the laws of the country and the right to run for elected office. As citizens they enjoy almost every right and privilege enjoyed by those who were born in this country. Each person assumes the responsibilities of upholding the Constitution of the United States, of participating in the tax system to allow for the operation of the government, and of living in accordance with the laws established by the government.

The government in the United States differs greatly from the governments of most of the other countries. In various governments today we see dictatorships, military juntas, monarchs, religious leaders, communist rule, socialist rule, etc. The government of the United States is a representative democracy determined by the election of the people. It is a government that in Lincoln's words is "of the people, by the people, and for the people."

When a person has had sufficient time to reflect on life in this new land and decides that he or she would like to become a citizen, that person begins the process. Classes are always available for those wishing to become citizens. The classes consist of the history of the United States and a study of the Constitution and laws of our country as well as an orientation to the process of government.

During this period of preparation the candidates have sponsors. These sponsors work with them during this period of preparation and accept a certain responsibility for them. The candidates are asked to obtain references from members of the community who have known them for a period of time. It is only after a preparation period of five years of residency that the candidates are eligible for citizenship. To become a citizen the candidates must take an examination to determine if they have sufficient knowledge about the history, law, and government of the country as well as a willingness to live up to the responsibilities of citizenship.

The day finally arrives when, accompanied by family and sponsors, the candidate appears at the Federal Courthouse and is sworn in as a citizen. Children born of that person are automatically granted citizenship. Part of the ceremony requires the person to pledge allegiance to the United States of America.

Thus, the new citizens initiated a desire to become a part of the country. Through this process they were able to become full participating members, enjoying all rights and privileges and assuming all responsibilities. And all of this was a free decision on the part of these new citizens.

The Church has many similar experiences. At this time let us look at the initiation of a person into the Christian community. The Church operates on a total "open door" policy. It welcomes a variety of peoples for a variety of reasons, asking only that they become one with the community through their belief in the life, death, and resurrection of Jesus Christ, their willingness to participate in the liturgical life of the Church, and their living the life of Christ.

These people have expressed their desire to belong. To belong to Church implies knowing something about it. It means to gain knowledge and to participate in the life of that Church. Of course, many ask to belong for a variety of wrong reasons. "It's the closest church to my house." "I like the discipline in the Catholic school." "They have a good-looking priest in the church." "It will give me a good image in my profession." "I like the ritual and processions." "They don't make too many demands on you." Part of the preparation process is to examine the reasons the person has and help the person deal with them.

Once it is determined that the person is sincerely motivated, the rights enjoyed and the responsibilities to be accepted as a member of the community are shared with the candidate. The candidate learns the structure of Church and the variety of gifts each member shares with the community. The word of God is shared to enable the candidate to gain insight into the Church's traditions, and time is spent on sharing that tradition.

The candidate is asked to select sponsors who because of their beliefs would be good teachers and examples to the person seeking entrance. The sponsors would be of special help to such candidates by enabling them to feel comfortable and secure in their decision of faith.

Ultimately the day arrives when the person has gained sufficient understanding and is prepared both interiorly and exteriorly to make a free decision in faith. This period of inquiry is known as the pre-catechumenate.

Before becoming citizens of the United States, people must be permanent residents for at least five years. The Church has its own period of "residency" known as the catechumenate. The Church has recently reintroduced the order of the catechumenate and the rite of the catechumenate as part of the initiation process. The period of time generally varies from two or three years. The catechumen is presented to the community and is accompanied by friends, acquaintances, family, and sponsors. During the period of the catechumenate, the catechumen is expected to live as much as possible the life of the Christian, study more deeply the teachings of the Church, and participate in the Mass during the liturgy of the Word. During this time, the catechumen should be nurtured by all the members of the faith community.

There are a number of ceremonies, rituals, and examinations within this catechumenate to enable the catechumen to live fully the life of a Christian. The final preparatory period, Lent, is almost like an extended retreat as catechumens prepare for their complete entry into the church.

The climax of the process of initiation occurs during the Easter vigil on Holy Saturday night. This is the most solemn night of the year, the night when we welcome into our midst the risen Lord, who in rising from the dead rescued us from the darkness of sin and brought us to a new life of the Father. Because of the significance of this night as we recall the paschal mystery, it has been, in the most ancient tradition of the Church, the night in which the catechumens are initiated into the Church through the sacraments of baptism, confirmation, and the Eucharist. (For more details, consult the introduction to the Rite for the Christian Initiation of Adults.)

The term "sacraments of initiation" has often been misunderstood. We have come to understand the sacraments through our reception of them. If you were asked to name the seven sacraments, you would easily be able to call them out like a shopping list: baptism, penance (confession), Eucharist (Holy Communion), confirmation, matrimony, holy orders, and anointing of the sick. They would be totally unrelated events that took place in your life.

In this unit we will cover in detail each of the sacraments of initiation. They are sacraments that are now and always have been tied together. The Church today very clearly expresses the need for us to understand baptism, confirmation, and the Eucharist as sacraments of initiation. In each of them we see people being brought to the full stature of Christ. Each of the sacraments frees us and enables us to carry out the mission of God in the Church and to the world.

Each baptized person becomes a child of God, a new creation through water and the power of the Holy Spirit. Those confirmed, having received the gift of the Holy Spirit, are strengthened, called to give witness to the world and to continue the work of building the body of Christ as they more perfectly image the Lord. The baptized also seek nourishment so that they may continue to live as children of God, give witness, and continually strive to build up the body of Christ in anticipation of the kingdom. This nourishment of the body and blood of Christ we call the Eucharist. Those who have been initiated through the reception of the sacraments of baptism, confirmation, and the Eucharist are responsible to pray for an ever greater outpouring of the Holy Spirit so that the whole race may be brought into the unity of God's family.

QUESTIONS FOR REFLECTION

1. Look at our country if you will for a moment. What are the origins of the people that make up your community?

2. What are your roots?

3. In what ways do others know that you belong?

2. BAPTISM

The scene is a parish church on a Sunday afternoon. The priest is busy locking up most of the doors of the church, leaving one open to allow people to make an afternoon visit to the Blessed Sacrament. He is anxious to get back to the rectory to catch the second half of the football game on TV.

Suddenly a car pulls up with three adults and a baby. The father of the child speaks up: "Father, I want my baby baptized. Do you have a few minutes?" The priest slowly nods his head and leads them to the sacristy, where he fills out the necessary information.

"Parish? Gee, Father, I'm afraid I don't remember. You see, we've only lived there six months, and I haven't found the church yet. But I've been a Catholic all my life, and no kid of mine is going to grow up without being a Catholic. Besides, you have a beautiful church here. It will look good in the pictures.

"Mother? Sure we're married. She's a Catholic like me. She couldn't make it here because she's getting ready for the christening party later on. There's a lot of preparation involved, you know.

"Godparents? That's why I have to do it today. Frank, what's your wife's name? Frank here was my old buddy from college. We don't see each other much. He's only in for the weekend. And you know what might happen if I wait too long."

So the football game must wait. The priest, having gotten all the necessary information, leads them to a corner in the back of the church. He lifts off the cover to the font and, in front of this container of stagnant water, begins the ritual of baptism. There are preliminary words, salt, and oil, but all are really waiting for the main event. Dipping a shell-shaped object into the water, the priest pours water over the head of the baby, saying: "Robert Howard, I baptize you in the name of the Father, and of the Son, and of the Holy Spirit." A few minor details, and the baptism is over. The four return home for the party, and the priest returns home for the fourth quarter.

That is how initiation into the Catholic Church occasionally used to take place. We realize that through such a ceremony a person truly is incorporated into the Church and becomes a part of the people of God. Yet, somehow, something is missing. The ritual is devoid of meaning. The symbols have become empty. The significance of Christian initiation has been lost.

> By baptism men are grafted into the paschal mystery of Christ; they die with him, are buried with him and rise with him. They receive the spirit of adoption as sons "in which we cry, Abba, Father" (Rom 8:15) and thus become true adorers such as the Father seeks (*Constitution on the Sacred Liturgy,* n. 6).

Through this sacrament we are incorporated into the Church. We are part of that people of God. Somehow this is related to our being "grafted into the paschal mystery of Christ." For this to occur, we must somehow die with Christ and rise with him. St. Paul shows us how, through the very ritual of baptism, we take part in the death and resurrection of Christ:

> Are you not aware that we who were baptized into Christ Jesus were baptized into his death? Through baptism into his death we were buried with him, so that, just as Christ was raised from the dead by the glory

of the Father, we too might live a new life. If we have been united with him through likeness to his death, so shall we be through a like resurrection (Rom 6:3–5).

What Paul is describing is not some ceremonial pouring of stagnant water over the head of a baby. He is describing the baptism of adults by immersion. "To baptize" means "to dip" or "to drown." The candidate was totally submerged under the water to symbolize death. The baptismal pool symbolizes the tomb in which Christ was buried. After saying the words, "I baptize you in the name of the Father, and of the Son, and of the Holy Spirit," the one baptizing raises the person from the water as the Father raised Christ from the tomb on Easter Sunday. A new life has occurred.

Because the candidate has received the same resurrected life as Christ, a life of the Father in the Spirit, he or she can indeed be called an adopted son or daughter. "In this sacred rite fellowship in Christ's death and resurrection is symbolized and brought about" (*Constitution on the Sacred Liturgy,* n. 7).

Once baptized, we share in the priesthood of Christ. This means that we have a right and an obligation to participate in any liturgical celebration. Christ the one high priest performs the offering, but along with us: it is an action of the whole Church, head and members. The bishops, priests, and deacons are a part of the ministerial or hierarchical priesthood. As Vatican II says:

> Though they differ essentially and not only in degree, the common priesthood of the faithful and the ministerial or hierarchical priesthood are nonetheless ordered one to another; each in its own proper way shares in the priesthood of Christ (*Constitution on the Church,* n. 10).

Since we have already discussed to a degree the initiation of adults, we shall direct our attention to the rite of infant baptism. For this rite to be rich in meaning it should follow the four basic principles for the reform of liturgy.

1. *Liturgy is an action of the whole body of the Church; it is not a private function.* As in the story related above, at one time the baptism of one's child was a private affair on a Sunday afternoon. Sometimes not even the mother was present. It is much more common today to find baptisms taking place within the Sunday liturgy. The child is not just being baptized; he or she is being initiated into this particular church, this parish community. The presence of the parish community indicates that it is a celebration of the whole community. They are welcoming the child into their midst.

2. *There must also be a proclamation of the Word of God.* Included as a part of the rite of infant baptism is a liturgy of the Word, including a homily. This exists whether the baptism is within Mass or not. Proclaiming the Word should not be the exclusive function of the priest; other members of the community are also to be involved.

3. The rite must be perceptible to the senses, for such is the nature of liturgy. The defect in the former rite of infant baptism was not the presence of symbols, but the presence of symbols that had lost their meaning. The reform of the rite attempted to use only symbols which conveyed what was taking place in the sacrament. Since baptism is a sharing in the paschal mystery, the Easter event, the paschal candle is to be lit during the ceremony. The mother, who with her husband is primarily responsible for raising the child, rather than the godmother, is to hold the child during the ceremony. The use of salt is now omitted, but the anointing on the breast of the child with oil has been retained together with a prayer explaining its significance. Fresh water is to be used each time, along with a prayer of blessing describing the life-giving effects of water throughout sacred history. Baptism by immersion is to be preferred. A second anointing with chrism takes place with a prayer explaining its relationship to the priesthood of Christ. The donning of the white baptismal robe and the lighting of a candle by the father from the paschal candle occur with an explanation of their relationship to the effects of baptism.

4. *It must be such that the people as a community can participate in it.* The reformed rite encourages singing and includes within itself ongoing dialogue between the priest and people. The people's response and acclamation at different points throughout the ceremony indicate their integral part in it.

Although the Rite for the Christian Initiation of Adults is said to be the norm, the presence of a Rite of Infant Baptism tells us that infant baptism is a practice that is to remain in the Church. What made the earlier story on infant baptism an account of such an empty ritual was the nearly magical way baptism was approached. To be a meaningful celebration, infant baptism must be seen in the context of adult initiation.

Were I to seek American citizenship for my child while at the same time not wishing to become a citizen myself, I would run into problems. If the American way of life means nothing to me, why should I want it for my child? In an even more important way, if the life of Christ is not important to me, why do I want it for my child? If I don't plan to live the life of Christ, how can I expect my child to do the same? If I am lacking in faith, how can I share with my child what I myself do not have?

A few years ago a story appeared in the paper about a woman whose pastor refused to baptize her baby because of her public opposition to the Church's position on abortion. Another priest, in defiance of the pastor, baptized the baby on the steps of the parish church. Without wishing to judge the woman, nonetheless a question arises: Why would she seek admittance of her child into a faith community with whom she is publicly at odds on a very crucial issue? Was the pastor being narrow-minded? Or was he being consistent to the meaning of initiation?

More and more parishes are requiring some catechesis of the parents before their child is baptized. Its purpose is to share with the parents the meaning of baptism as a sacrament of initiation and to enable them to understand clearly their responsibilities in having their child incorporated into the Catholic Church. This catechesis provides a wonderful opportunity for the parents to examine their own faith life, so that they may realize more clearly how they will be able to share that faith.

QUESTIONS FOR REFLECTION

1. As a member of your local faith community (parish) what is your responsibility for the infants as well as adults being baptized there?

2. How would you see these baptisms as nourishing your own faith?

3. In your opinion what are the implications of a change in emphasis from an "original sin washing" to a "communal initiation"?

4. When you ask the Church to baptize your child or godchild, what are you telling the Church that you are going to do?

3. CONFIRMATION

Even some of the most well planned vacations can turn into frustrating experiences. Money is set aside; the place is selected after much deliberation; the vacation schedule is arranged; a hotel is selected, and reservations are made well in advance of the trip to assure proper and adequate housing. The day before departure the clothes are laid out for packing. Anxiety begins to build up.

Finally you board the plane and settle down with a thousand thoughts about your trip. Thought number one is to get set up at the hotel so that you will be foot-loose and fancy-free. The hotel car is at the airport; you enter it and are whisked from the airport directly to the hotel. Upon arrival at the desk to register, the nervous clerk informs you that no reservations have been made. After a not-so-polite hassle, you are informed that the hotel is packed with conventioneers. You talk until you are blue in the face and get nowhere. Suddenly the manager arrives and asks if you had confirmation of your reservation. You reply: "What do you mean when you say 'confirmation'?"

We refer to receiving the Holy Spirit in the sacrament of confirmation. This reception of the Holy Spirit was also part of our baptism. It would seem that once we receive the Holy Spirit in baptism, we continue our life with the Holy Spirit as part of it. Why then are we receiving the Holy Spirit at confirmation? To many it would seem redundant. This is one of the reasons we hear people asking the same question over and over, "What do you mean when you say 'confirmation'?" To respond to the question we would have to say that the Spirit is indeed given in baptism. The Spirit received in confirmation is in fact more of the same. Karl Rahner asserts that the Church has already given us the Word in baptism, but it says it even *more* distinctly and more urgently in the word of grace of confirmation whereby our freedom is again awakened and gently invited to choose life. The General Introduction to the Rite of Christian Initiation says:

> Signed with the gift of the Spirit in confirmation, Christians *more* perfectly become the images of their Lord and are filled with the Holy Spirit. They bear witness to him before all the world and eagerly work for building up the body of Christ (n. 2).

Confirmation fully understood is the reaffirmation of the value of the individual. To be confirmed involves personal choice and a sense of commitment. We unite with the "body of Christ," the people of God, but are sealed with the Holy Spirit as an individual. Strengthened by the Spirit we are called to go forth and live out our faith.

Confirmation is not an ending or a completion. It is rather a beginning. It is that beginning to image more perfectly our Lord, giving witness and working toward the building up of the body of Christ.

Confirmation demands not a passive recipient but one capable of seeing, hearing, and understanding what is happening and why it is happening, and of freely accepting it.

Confirmation is a call from the Spirit. But there must be a willingness, openness, and awareness to accept the call. Only in this acceptance does there exist the ongoing process of becoming a Christian.

Confirmation is a challenge to each recipient to give witness to the world of the life-styles and values revealed to us by Jesus and to be able to make them known to others through the gifts of the Spirit working in our lives.

Perhaps the greatest misunderstanding in regard to confirmation occurs when people discuss postponement of the sacrament until a person is capable of making a conscious and wholehearted commitment to Christ. This discussion is centered around the sacrament of baptism, not confirmation. At baptism the parents and Church promise that they will give the infant love and example so that he or she will be gradually drawn to full commitment to Christ. No new sacrament is needed for this. Confirmation has not been, is not, and never was intended to be the sacrament of adult commitment.

Confirmation is then the perfecting of baptized Christians who are now commissioned through this sacrament to act in the name of Christ, to act as Christ acted, for the same end that Christ acted. The Christian is now asked not only to offer praise and worship, but is sent to the world with a mission to preach the Gospel to and for all people. Mature Christians are confirmed Christians—those who have confirmed their baptismal promises, spoken for themselves in accepting the Church, and have new life in Christ. The Spirit is given to Christians at baptism, and now they receive the fullness of the Spirit, as the apostles did, to carry out the work of making known the salvation of the world.

QUESTIONS FOR REFLECTION

1. How do you show the strength of your commitment to your membership in some group or organization?

2. How do you see the relationship between confirmation as a sacrament of initiation and as an impetus to commitment?

3. What are the problems connected with catechesis for the sacrament of confirmation? How is your diocese resolving them?

4. EUCHARIST

Personalized license plates are a popular item in some states. For $25 plus an annual fee of $15 a person can have one's own special message on the plates, provided it does not exceed seven digits, is not anything obscene, and has not already been taken. One woman has on the plates of her Volkswagen: LUKE 24. If you are at all curious, you will find that this final chapter of Luke's Gospel relates the post-resurrection experience of Jesus. Since the stories are about the *risen* Lord, they also indicate to us how we might encounter the risen Lord.

The story which likely relates most directly to us is the one about the two disciples on the road to Emmaus on Easter Sunday (Lk 24:13–35). As they were walking, Jesus appeared in their midst, but they failed to recognize him. Even when they recounted to Jesus the events of the past few days, they still didn't recognize him. Jesus then began to explain the Scriptures to them, saying that the crucifixion was not an ending but the prelude to the resurrection and that all of this occurred in fulfillment of the Scriptures. Even then they failed to recognize Jesus. When did recognition come?

> When he had seated himself with them to eat, he took bread, pronounced the blessing, then broke the bread and began to distribute it to them. With that their eyes were opened and they recognized him (vv. 30–31).

It was only in the breaking of bread that the disciples really recognized Jesus. Whenever the term "breaking of bread" is used in the New Testament, it refers to the Eucharist. Note the similarity of words used by Jesus in both the meal on the road to Emmaus and at the Last Supper when Jesus instituted the Eucharist.

> Then taking bread and giving thanks, he broke it and gave it to them, saying: "This is my body to be given for you. Do this as a remembrance of me." He did the same with the cup after eating, saying as he did so: "This cup is the new covenant in my blood, which will be shed for you" (Lk 22:19–20).

This is what the celebration of the Eucharist, the Mass, is about. The Mass, the Lord's supper, is simultaneously and inseparably a sacrifice in which the sacrifice of the cross is perpetuated, a memorial of the death and resurrection of Christ, and a sacred banquet in which we are offered under the appearance of bread and wine the body and blood of Christ (*Eucharisticum Mysterium,* May 25, 1967). On Calvary, Christ alone was the priest offering and the victim offered to the heavenly Father. At Mass it is the entire body of Christ. We are the priest; we are the victim. In the chapter on liturgy, we already saw how we as a community celebrate the memorial of the death and resurrection of Christ. We shall soon see how the Eucharist is a sacred banquet.

When we studied the rite of initiation we saw that complete initiation into the Church involves three sacraments: baptism, confirmation, and the Eucharist. The first two are only received once because initiation is a unique event. But we constantly celebrate the Eucharist so that we may strengthen the commitment we made when we entered the Church. When we are first initiated we are like newborn babies. We need constant nourishment for our faith to grow.

Eating the body and blood of Christ in the Eucharist is our nourishment to strengthen our original commitment. The *Constitution on the Church* says:

> Really sharing in the body of the Lord in the breaking of the eucharistic bread, we are taken up into communion with him and with one another. "Because the bread is one, we, though many, are one body, all of us who partake of the one bread" (1 Cor 10:17). In this way all of us are made members of his body (cf. 1 Cor 12:27), "but severally members one of another" (Rom 12:4) (n. 7).

If you break bread together you are sharing it. Jesus' life was shared and given up for us. When we break bread in the name of Jesus, it is not merely Jesus' sharing his life for us; it is our sharing our lives for one another. The more we are willing to share with one another, the more effectively we are building up our community of faith. That too is bound to have an effect on others around us. We share our goods, our friends, our ideas, our ideals, our food, our clothes. And permeating all this is the presence of Jesus who made this possible. He gave us his life, and through his life we come together.

During the Second World War a Nazi pilot was shot down over enemy territory. He was seriously injured, so an ambulance immediately rushed him to a first aid station. The man had lost a lot of blood and was in need of a blood transfusion immediately, but he refused. Why? He demanded only pure Aryan blood. They told him that without the needed blood he would die, but they could not give him pure Aryan blood. The man continued to refuse a transfusion, and as a result he died.

How important is the Eucharist to our life? Just about as important as the blood was to the dying Nazi. To see how important Jesus considered the Eucharist, we need only turn to the sixth chapter of John's Gospel where Jesus delivers his great discourse on the bread of life. Earlier in the chapter Jesus had miraculously multiplied the loaves for the five thousand people to eat, and people were following him to get more of the same. But Jesus offered something even greater: himself.

> I myself am the living bread come down from heaven. If anyone eats this bread he shall live forever; the bread I will give is my flesh, for the life of the world (Jn. 6:51).

To eat one's flesh meant cannibalism and to drink blood was absolutely repugnant to a Jew. Jesus' listeners challenged his statement. But Jesus even more emphatically tells us:

> Let me solemnly assure you, if you do not eat the flesh of the Son of Man and drink his blood, you have no life in you. He who feeds on my flesh and drinks my blood has life eternal and I will raise him up on the last day. For my flesh is real food and my blood real drink. The man who feeds on my flesh and drinks my blood remains in me, and I in him. Just as the Father who has life sent me and I have life because of the Father, so the man who feeds on me will have life because of me. This is the bread that came down from heaven. Unlike your ancestors who ate and died nonetheless, the man who feeds on this bread shall live forever (Jn. 6:53–58).

In the Eucharist Christ's body is whole and entire, for he is risen and glorified. Therefore in eating the bread we are consuming the body and blood of Christ. In drinking the cup we are consuming the body and blood of Christ. Because there is a much deeper meaning for us in both eating the bread and drinking the cup, the practice of receiving Communion under both species is preferred, although not necessary. As Paul says:

> Is not the cup of blessing we bless a sharing in the blood of Christ? And is not the bread we break a sharing in the body of Christ? Because the loaf of bread is one, we, many though we are, are one body, for we all partake of one loaf (1 Cor 10:16–17).

There is a very real connection between the body of Christ which we receive in the Eucharist and the body of Christ which is the Church. It is simply present in a different way. Our faith demands that we show equal reverence to both. Mother Teresa of Calcutta once told her sisters that the Holy Hour is made by them each morning out of a devotion to the body of Christ present in the Eucharist. When they go out to minister to the person who is lice-infested, diseased, foul-smelling because of decayed flesh, and dying, that person is to be given the same devotion because he or she is indeed the body of Christ. A Eucharist not lived out is a sacrilege. "Whoever eats the bread or drinks the cup unworthily sins against the body and blood of the Lord" (1 Cor 11:27).

The relationship of the Eucharist to life has never been more clearly expressed than by a young dedicated Christian living the life of radical poverty. His reflections:

> While awaiting the fall of the corrupt working ruling class which for me also included the Church, this Catholic Worker stuff seemed okay. Everything they did appealed to my young radical heart: feeding poor people, visiting the jail, resisting the war. But why all of this Catholic stuff? Why the Mass? Why the prayers? Why call it the Catholic Work-

er. Why not the radical anarcho-syndicalist Worker? What the hell does Catholic have to do with revolution?

With each passing day it became clearer why Dorothy Day, the founder of the Worker movement, had forsaken her Marxist friends and converted to Catholicism. It's not that she was no longer radical; she simply found deeper roots for her radicalism and a home for her spiritual longings.

Within the context of the Worker much of the absurdity of Catholicism began to make sense. We spent our days as we still do, preparing and serving a meal to hundreds of men and women on skid row. Exhausted, we would gather at the end of the week to celebrate an informal Eucharist. It was all so clear and simple.

Christ meant the Eucharist to be a symbol of our lives. Just as Christ sacrificed his life for us and feeds us with his body, so we also sacrifice ourselves and feed the poor. This is what we celebrate, that through our sacrifices the broken body of humanity can become one in Christ.

The great sin of Catholicism is to confuse substance and form. The sacraments of the Church are such beautiful symbols in and of themselves, that the substance, which is our daily lives of service, is lost and we slip into idolatry.

At last I was home. There was no longer any distinction between our daily lives of service to the poor and our communion with Christ in the Eucharist. My radicalism truly had roots. Now it could take hold and flourish. While other young radicals fell by the wayside as their notions of the Woodstock nation faded, I had the strength to struggle for a greater kingdom. Certainly I have derived great comfort and strength from my reunion with the Church (Jeff Dietrich, "A Vision of the Church as Mother of the Poor," *Catholic Agitator,* January 1979, p. 2).

QUESTIONS FOR REFLECTION

1. Examine various catechetical programs in your parish for different age levels (e.g. graded courses of study, youth ministry, Scripture study, catechesis). Do they address the needs of the learners according to their individual stages of readiness? List the signs._____

_____

_____

_____

_____

2. Examine yourself. What is your stage of faith development at this time? List the signs._____

_____

_____

3. Are there programs in your parish that meet your needs? Describe them and tell how they meet your needs. If not, what program might meet your needs?
_____

4. Interview some persons at the level at which you plan to teach. What characteristics do you observe in them?_____

Unit Five

DEVELOPMENT OF THE PERSON

1. STAGES OF GROWTH AND OF READINESS FOR THE MESSAGE

The joy and excitement of a husband and wife at the birth of a child is perhaps the happiest moment of their lives. The expression of love that is represented and the period of waiting, anticipating and preparing for the birth are times when the couple reflect on their lives together and dream of what is to be for their child. From the moment of conception to the birth a growth process has taken place.

If you have ever seen a collection of fetuses in a laboratory or doctor's office, you may have noticed the development that takes place over the weeks. You see hands formed, fingernails appear, toes develop, hair grow, and facial features become clear. This growth process does not end at birth but rather becomes a lifelong process of the development of the person. While we are able to observe the physical growth that is taking place, we must be aware that at the same time a psychological, emotional, and intellectual growth has also begun and will continue in the person.

To understand human growth and development, one must consider that it is a cradle-to-grave process through which each person must pass. The stages for this development are the same for each person; however, the process is gradual. All people move at different times from one stage to the other at their own rate of speed. That which has been experienced by them as they go through each phase contributes to their developing personality and will have a marked effect on their behavior. To force them into a learning process beyond their level of development could prove futile and even harmful to them.

In a first grade classroom on the opening day of school we see a variety of responses from the six-year-old children. Some eagerly burst into the room and begin to explore its many treasures, seemingly unaware of the presence of teacher or parent. Others quietly enter the room with a guarded eye on their parents but take a seat and wait quietly. Still others begin to cry, desperately hang on to their parent, refuse to take a seat, and show little, if any, interest in the room, its treasures, the teacher, or other students. Each of the three descriptions has a history. First, we would have to look at the environment that surrounded each student prior to this day.

The first grouping has been involved in a nursery school for two years and attended a pre-school kindergarten this past year. These children have spent a considerable amount of time with many others of the same age. They were made to feel secure outside the atmosphere of the family, were encouraged to share and work with other children in group situations, and discovered that making friends was an enjoyable thing to do. They are quite aware of the excitement that can be found in a classroom situation and readily adapt.

The children quietly and guardedly entering the room have been told by other brothers and sisters about school. They have experienced the many things the other children in the family have made and brought home from school. Without a doubt they have often been the students as older brothers and sisters have whiled away hours in playing school at home. The thought of being taken from the comfort of the "nest" and placed in the classroom has a great deal of the unknown for such children. However, trust has been built with the experiences of other family members, and, slowly, but most assuredly, they will adapt and succeed in conquering this new situation.

Those who cry and cling to a parent have not been used to many environments except the security of home. Other children, a strange atmosphere, the teacher, and thoughts of the parent leaving them are more than these six-year-olds can deal with. They will experience difficulty in adjusting to a new situation, and the teacher will be required to show great patience until they are able to trust and feel secure.

The three types of students have been conditioned by their surroundings. Their uniqueness and individuality are clearly expressed. In common they are each six years old, entering first grade, and physically developing at somewhat the same pace. Our presumption would be to deal with each in the same manner. As teachers we have our lesson plan, textbooks, and materials to work with. However, our first consideration must be the student. The teacher entering a classroom extremely confident of the material to be taught and yet not knowing the students or understanding them as individuals is asking for failure.

In the area of growth and development from infancy to adulthood, much has been written. We can find a profile of the six-year-old or the forty-five-year-old person. The stages fit general areas, and persons in these stages fit somewhere within the wide curve. To look at any group and assess them based on the various stages where the group is to be found has created disaster for many a catechist. To use the stages as a guide is wise, but assessing the uniqueness of each individual in one's group will present a much clearer portrait of those with whom the catechist will be working.

To make this individual assessment we should come to understand people by finding out about their physical and intellectual development, their attitudes and interests, their concept of self, their environment and the needs that affect them. A catechist can begin this type of assessment by asking the student to respond to the following survey:

1. Five things I like to do . . .
2. Two things I do very well . . .
3. I am afraid to . . .
4. My favorite sports activity is . . .
5. My parents . . .
6. My best friends are . . .

Although this is not an exhaustive look at what makes the students "tick," it does give the catechist some insights into their feelings and attitudes. It most certainly would enable the catechist to approach the students with some understanding of who they are and where they are at. One must recognize each person as a whole, integrated, individual being who has been somewhere and is going somewhere, rather than a person who has remained stationary. Catechists must never assume that they are the first persons the students have encountered in their lived experience.

From the many studies printed for various age levels, it has been determined that characteristics of people can be placed in general categories. These characteristics relate to the abilities a person possesses at a given time. As a catechist, one who shares a religious message, it is necessary to understand how much and in what ways the religious message is understandable and relevant in the lives of the students. The following should give the catechist an overview of the various levels of development along with the religious readiness at each of the levels.

THE PRIMARY CHILD

Characteristics

Primary children learn primarily from their own world. Such learning is centered in home, family and love experiences. They are interested primarily in the concrete world, the "real" that surrounds them in their everyday experiences. Such children cannot handle abstract thoughts or concepts.

Theirs is the world of "me," and much of their life is lived in the "me" world. They are self-centered,

Religion Readiness

Introduce primary children to the "family of God" through their experiences with their own family. A relationship can be developed with Jesus as a brother who loves us and leads us to the Father. Introduce concepts of right and wrong, choices, and expressions of sorrow in preparation for the sacrament of penance. Speak of food in context of a meal with family. Include special meals and celebrations, e.g., Easter, Christmas, birthday.

striving always to be the center of attention, and they exhibit little, if any, interest in working at group activities.

A variety of learning experiences is vital. Their attention span is quite limited (approximately ten minutes). Teaching must include bodily activities and should include music.

All the senses must be incorporated in the learning experience. The primary child needs to touch, taste, feel, smell, and hear, and to have the whole body involved in the learning experiences.

Food can be introduced as nourishment and life-giving as preparation for the Eucharist.

Touch these students with God's love. Use the creation that surrounds them as examples of God's love. This may include trees used for shade and building houses, water for cleaning and drinking, air for breathing, flowers for beauty, vegetables for eating, and animals for pleasure as well as food.

Clarifications are needed at this time for primary children. Very often their concept of God is the "endless gift giver," a Santa Claus of sorts. It is important for the teacher to give correct examples of God, using as a source the many examples that are present to the lived experience of the child.

THE INTERMEDIATE CHILD

Intermediate children are working at developing their own attitudes that are independent of adults. They are discarding childish patterns of behavior. However, they can fluctuate a great deal. It is a period of transition and can be extremely difficult for these children. We see an inconsistency in their conduct, and they tend to be disorganized. They are very sensitive and moody at times and are often quite restless.

This is a period of time when they are beginning to develop their own friends. They seem to select their own group. Competition in group experiences is well handled by intermediate children. They work well with teams and are quite loyal both to their group and to their family. The worship of heroes is a prime motivator. They can tell you in a minute their favorite ball player or television idol.

Their attention span is longer than that for the primary child (approximately twenty minutes). Memorization of detail is possible. They see the details more clearly than the main ideas. They are basically interested in the concrete, not the abstract.

Intermediate children are collectors and builders of models. They spend hours with stamps, rocks, pictures, or collections of any kind. An increase of their ability in their tool skills, especially reading, is very noticeable.

The catechist must recognize the inconsistent behavior practices as part of the students' growth process, maintaining a long-range view of intermediate children to see them through this transitional period.

The catechist must maintain a sense of humor while at the same time setting clear limits on behavior. Don't take strange behavior personally; however, be firm in handling the situation.

These years are great for introducing the characters of the Old Testament. Journal projects, diaries, and travelogues would be of particular interest at this age level. They are quite capable of working on art projects, such as building model cities, making murals or collages, booklets, etc. They are capable of games (drill exercises) that consist of boys' teams versus girls' teams.

These children are able to deal with Jesus through the here-and-now. Research of daily news items that relate to Jesus can be found, shared, and discussed. Biblical people can be introduced as the heroes of the time, and the students will be able to recognize people in their lived experiences that correlate.

Discussion of doctrinal formulas with the students so that they may understand enables them to memorize the material. Once they are given the data necessary, they are quite able to explore on their own. Supplementary materials should be available because they will do research on their own and submit reports of their findings.

As groups they can be channeled into preparing posters, charts, maps, and banners, and into role playing on a religious theme.

THE JUNIOR HIGH STUDENT

Junior high students are at a difficult time in their life. Much is happening at this growth period physically, mentally, and emotionally. Boys are about two years behind girls in this process. They are extremely sensitive about being different. They develop deep close friendships with peers of the same sex. It is at this point that they begin to experience the awakening of sexual awareness.

An ability to reason is being acquired, and they begin to question authority. They are no longer content with "yes" or "no" answers. They need a great deal of time spent in clarifying rights and wrongs. They have acquired the ability to handle abstract concepts at this age.

Peer relationships are extremely important to the students. They feel secure with their peers and will conform to the group. They can become negative and antagonistic to adult authority. They accept and participate in fads in order to be accepted by the group. Much love and support is needed by these students in spite of their inability to respond. This is the age of searching for self-image. It is at times difficult for these students to determine whether they are children or adults.

They are capable of dealing with history in a new sense. They have acquired the ability to think chronologically. They need to be needed, are service oriented, and want to be useful to society. They have a strong sense of social justice.

Each catechist teaching at this level must understand the students' inability to be totally involved. One must accept their restlessness, moodiness, boredom, and awkwardness. They tend to become "dreamy" as a result of the rapid spurts of growth that are taking place. Through their developed friendships it is possible to introduce the student to the person of Jesus Christ. The parish community can be given as an example of friendship.

Work with these students to go beyond the surface answers of childhood as part of their experience of growing to adulthood as a Christian. Deal calmly and reasonably with their challenge to authority. Use that challenge to show how necessary it is for people to act responsibly in the Church today. Help them to accept authority and the misuse of authority as a fact of life.

Help these students to experience Christ's deep love for them as individuals. Enable them to see their personal faith dimension. Show them that you care about them and understand their situation. Show them that your caring for them is not dependent on their behavior but rather because you accept them as Christ accepts each of us. Encourage them to explore, treating them in accordance with the role they are trying out.

Be impartial, just, and patient. Understand that most open attempts at affection will be rejected. As you exhibit impartiality, patience, and justice, call them to become just persons. Help them to find ways to become a part of the social apostolate, serving others as Christ did. Show the Church as being real in the world of the 1980's and relevant in our lives. Christ calls each of us to live and love as Christians. Show the students that they can be this kind of Christian. Encourage them to search the Scriptures. Have them look at the early Christian communities to see what served to build and what served to destroy. Then have them make their analogies with the present-day world.

Deal with them on issues of social justice. These issues can be on the national, state, city, neighborhood, parish, or class level. Allow them to discuss ways in which they could work to alleviate the conditions. Use examples from the New Testament to find solutions.

THE HIGH SCHOOL STUDENT

Self-image is very important to adolescents. They spend much time taking stock of themselves. The extraverted actions of junior high students change to an introverted tendency as adolescents begin to look at themselves.

At this age young people can be extremely cynical at times and then in the next moment become idealistic. They spend time in looking at the world that surrounds them. They are very alert to double standards, conflict and justice. At this time they often become part of a bandwagon for various causes that might gain their interest.

Such young persons are very sensitive and insecure. Because of this lack of security and sensitivity they tend to seek others who are understanding, accepting and affectionate. What other adolescents think is very important to them as they work to establish a position within the peer group.

Adolescents are capable of deep thinking. They spend much time reasoning out a situation and can be logical in working through a problem. Nothing is what it appears to be to adolescents. They tend to analyze most things. On occasion they will make snap judgments and are taken by anything that smacks of sensationalism.

High school students must know that they are important to you. A catechist must be concerned and care about each student as an individual. The students must be able to experience this love and concern. In this way the catechist can explore Christ and his love and concern for each of us as individuals.

Provide ways for adolescents to work at developing their self-image. This must be accomplished by the catechist allowing for freedom in the students' expression. Often they will give the appearance of turning off any adult direction. By "hanging in there" one will discover that what was being said by the adult was being absorbed by the students and weighed against their own ideas as they pertain to their specific needs.

The catechist must be a strong witness of his or her beliefs. A positive outlook (and we don't mean a head-in-the-clouds approach) about people, the world, the local community and the parish community will enable adolescents to recognize that goodness is present. In this context the catechist is able to encourage students to accept Christ and to see in him the perfect person with whom to identify.

Students at this level will question and challenge as they arrive at moments of crises in their faith. Accept the questioning and challenges. Be honest if you don't have all the ready answers or rebuttals. It will be all right with the students. This honesty makes you acceptable and believable. Test the intellect of the students. Challenge them by insisting that they think and reason for themselves. Don't be ready with "pat answers" for all your questions. This questioning and challenging will help them to commit themselves freely to Christ.

THE ADULT LEARNER

To understand adults and their needs in education we must discontinue trying to approach each adult at the same level. If we say that education is a cradle-to-grave process, we must accept the fact that adults are learners. All learners are unique and are not at the same place. It is of utmost importance to anyone working with adults to assess effectively the needs of the group. Only in this way can one determine the variety of people and the places from which they are coming.

One working with adults must take a good look at the group. They represent a variety of life-styles, and any effectively communicated message must take this into consideration. Any group of adults today could consist of married people, people with families grown, people with families starting, divorced situations, single persons who have elected not to marry, senior citizens, young adults, and single-parent families.

Today we find many who have not updated their religious thinking from the days of their youth. They may have completed their religious education at their confirmation or before. For these people many changes have taken place in the Church. We must be sensitive to the approaches we take with these people. Others may have accomplished considerable reading and in some ways moved along with the changes in the Church. Some have sought and are working in a variety of educational settings from parish religious education programs through college-level study programs of enrichment. At the same time large numbers are confused and turned off by what has happened in the Church in recent years. They are often resentful because they feel a great loss of security or identification with the community.

As "Church," we must accept the responsibility for removing parents from the role of religion teacher or sharer of faith for their families. We have lived a long history of instilling in parents that "Sister" or "Father" have the answers. We encouraged them to abdicate the responsibility for the educational/catechetical process of their children and give it to the "Church." Today we are attempting to hand it back to the parents, who are at times frightened, who feel inadequate, and who at times become resentful because their preparation to handle the job has fallen so far short of the goal.

After a proper needs assessment of the group is made, programs tailored to fit the needs of the various groups can be explored. These might include a course on the documents of Vatican II, a Scripture course, discussion groups on religious topics of interest, prayer, an updating on the understanding of sacraments, a series of enrichment talks on a variety of subjects, and a study of liturgy.

Develop a program that would enable the various groups within the Church to participate. These groups could include senior citizens or single parents. What type program would enable them to feel part of the Church? You might include various speakers who would be able to respond to the various needs of the group. Perhaps you could form support groups for those in need.

Plan programs that will meet the needs of people at various educational levels. Every parish has its own resources. Look for those who are in the process of seeking religious education from special programs or who have been studying at the college level. These people, found within the community, are the ones who are able to work with the people who have had little or no updating to this time. They are non-threatening; they have an appreciation of where the people are coming from and would be sensitive to them. At all times we must respect where the learners are coming from if we are to enable them to learn. All too often we are ready to present in heavy, theological language material that the learners are incapable of understanding. Here again the tendency is to get Father to do it. With the best motivation in the world, Father often comes prepared to present material that the group is not ready for. This happens because the persons responsible for the program have not shared sufficiently with Father about the group he will be working with. When this happens we only serve to confuse people to a greater degree.

Make a concerted effort to work with the parents. This is not to suggest that we "dump" the religious education of the child in favor of adult education. Rather, at this time in the Church, parents should be encouraged and aided in their desire to work with their children. Our programs should be reflecting a variety of ways for parents to become part of the team that is working with their children. Sacramental preparation is a wonderful opportunity for this type of activity. Parents are enthusiastic and interested in what their child is learning. Invite them to see what is being done and encourage their support in the home for what you are doing. Invite them to evenings of enrichment that will enable them to feel comfortable with what is taking place. Offer examples of things they might do in the home with their child. Encourage them to work and plan the celebration that will take place. Recognize and appreciate that they are working people who are involved in many activities and responsible for supporting a family and that at times the meeting date and time is not convenient for them. Know that they want the best for their child. Appreciate that they are the first educators of their child. Above all, recognize that they come from a variety of different circumstances. Allow for the differences that will surely occur. Often it is through a sharing of differences that we all grow. And be the witness that Christ would be: accept their unique gifts, accept these people in love, and you will find them extremely grateful for all you do in his name.

Stages of Growth and Development of Adults

It is apparent from what was said above about adults and adult education that in dealing with learners there are myriads of models and programs. The people's background is so diverse that it does not do justice to generalize without clearly assessing the learners of each program. When one speaks of stages of growth and development of the adult, this must be understood in broad general terms. Much is being written in this area today, and most writers make it very clear that their studies are not conclusive.

Early Adulthood

Within these years an individual seeks independence from family ties. This begins with completion of high school. Such people may begin to seek work and obtain separate living accommodations or may go away to college or enter military service. During these years they begin to make their own decisions. Often rebelling against anything that would reflect home or family, the young adult may also drift away from the Church.

A serious testing of adulthood takes place in these years. During this time there may occur serious consideration of one's life, marriage, and the starting of a family, or a vocation to religious life. In these years new friends are found. These are times of vision and dreaming. At this age people find little need for a dependence on God.

Around the age of thirty adults encounter questions about the direction and meaning of life. They have had enough experience as an adult to become aware of God's gift of his Son. It is at this time that a genuine adult spirituality can be awakened.

Middle Adulthood

The beginning years are times of settling down. People tend to focus on raising children or succeeding in their jobs. They begin to develop a new relationship with their parents, looking at the many ways they are so alike. Because adults at this level are involved with job and family, they tend to feel somewhat unfulfilled. Their primary focus is providing for the family or caring for the children.

Somewhere in their late thirties or early forties a change takes place in the orientation of such persons. They come to the realization that they will not fulfill the dreams of their youth. They arrive at an understanding of their limitations and the limitations of others. When viewed in terms of how much longer they have to live, at this stage they can often become frustrated or angry. Because of this awareness they often turn to God, seeking fulfillment in him.

Following this crisis many adults are able through faith to find new meaning and direction in their lives. Children are leaving home, and many people take this time to get involved in outside activities or look to second careers. It is a time when the demands of family are lessened, allowing time for them to explore their creativity.

In the early to middle fifties adults become accepting of their limitations and are able to quell the inner turmoil and find peace. Friendship is important, and adults at this age want to share in the fullness of Christian community.

Later Adulthood

One must accept at this stage aging as a natural process. It is at this time that people must come to grips with their physical selves and their necessary limitations. Generally, during this period people are faced with retirement. Time must be taken to work through this experience and how it will affect their lives.

This often has been called the age of integration. It is that time when one must come to terms in integrating the whole of one's life.

People in these years have much free time, since less demands are placed upon them. In light of their many years of lived experience they have a wealth to share. Growing in faith is a lifelong process, and those in later adulthood should seek to share their faith experience as they continue this process of growth.

QUESTIONS FOR REFLECTION

1. At what stage of your life do you feel you were ready to make a lasting commitment? What were the signs that told you that?

2. What did you have to go through ahead of time before you were able to make a commitment? _____
_____
_____
_____
_____

3. In light of this, why would confirmation be considered a sacrament of initiation rather than a sacrament of commitment? _____
_____
_____
_____
_____

2. SACRAMENTS OF COMMITMENT

A person can say over and over again "I love you," but in the end it is one's deeds that really show it. A person can say over and over "Yes, I'll do whatever you say," but only one's actions really indicate actual obedience. Jesus likewise is to be judged primarily not by what he said but by what he did. We may say that Jesus loves us. We may say that he was obedient to the Father. But unless we see by Jesus' deeds that he really loves us and was obedient to the Father, his words mean nothing.

Jesus himself said: "There is no greater love than this: to lay down one's life for one's friends" (Jn 15:13). And Jesus did precisely that: he laid down his life for us on the cross. Jesus also said: "It is not to do my own will that I have come down from heaven, but to do the will of him who sent me" (Jn 6:39). Speaking of his death Jesus said:

> My soul is troubled now,
> yet what should I say—
> Father, save me from this hour?
> But it was for this that I came to this hour.
> Father, glorify your name (Jn 12:27–28).

By dying on the cross, Jesus was accepting the will of the Father. It was Jesus' action that indicated his works. The paschal mystery, Christ's sacrificial offering on the cross and rising to glory, is the central mystery of our redemption. Each sacrament somehow is a celebration and recapitulation of the paschal mystery. Christ's saving action becomes present. To be a Christian is to live out that paschal mystery in our daily lives. Jesus said to all: "Whoever wishes to be my follower must deny his very self, take up his cross each day, and follow in my steps" (Lk 9:23).

Daily carrying the cross in sacrifice for others is part of being a Christian. It is to live out that mystery into which one was initiated through baptism, confirmation, and the Eucharist. Although these sacraments of initiation call for Christians to live out their commitment, there are some sacraments that symbolize this commitment and presume a level of Christian maturity. They call for the person to be a living sign of the paschal mystery. In light of this, these sacraments could appropriately be called sacraments of commitment. There are two such sacraments: matrimony and holy orders.

In matrimony a Christian man and woman pledge their lifelong commitment of love and fidelity to each other in marriage. In holy orders a man pledges his lifelong commitment to be a spiritual leader of the Church. Without these people having a certain maturity of faith and deep commitment of purpose, the sacrament cannot be effectively carried out. They are called to be and to live out the sacrament which they receive.

MATRIMONY

Love stories seem to have a universal appeal. One of the most famous love stories is Shakespeare's *Romeo and Juliet.* Those two young people were madly in love with each other. However, Romeo came from the house of Montague, and Juliet was a Capulet. The two families were always feuding. Neither side wanted the two to marry, and Juliet's family had her closely guarded to prevent the couple from eloping. Finally Juliet took a sleeping potion to make it appear that she was dead. Her plan was that after being taken to the tomb, she would awaken, slip away, and marry Romeo. However, Romeo found her and, believing her dead, killed himself. Juliet, upon awaking, follows his example. Over the bodies of their dead children the two families reconcile. This is a tragic story but a beautiful one of the love of two people. That same theme has been successfully repeated in plays and movies like *West Side Story*.

What makes this theme popular is that love is such a common human experience. It is one of the deepest human needs and strongest emotions. From the Scriptures we find another love story, that of Hosea and Gomer. Gomer was nothing more than a prostitute, yet Hosea loved her and married her. Though she was unfaithful, Hosea never relented in his love, devotion, and fidelity to her. This story is the basis for God's revelation of how much he loves his people Israel. Hosea symbolizes God, and Gomer represents Israel. Despite Israel's infidelity, her idolatry, God never relents in his love for Israel.

In Jesus we see a deeper love than even Hosea exemplified. Jesus' entire life was so directed that we might experience the love of God and share in his life. Jesus was the living sacrament of the love of God. Every action of his—especially his death on the cross—revealed to us how loving God is. Love in its deepest and truest sense is God.

>Love, then, consists in this:
>not that we have loved God,

but that he has loved us
and has sent his Son as an offering for our sins (1 Jn 4:10).

God is love,
and he who abides in love
abides in God,
and God in him (1 Jn 4:16).

Marriage as a social contract has been a part of human history. We saw how God used an existing situation, the story of Hosea and Gomer, to reveal how deeply he loved Israel. He has done something similar with marriage. He has raised marriage to the dignity of a sacrament to enable the world to know what love really is. The love of a husband and wife is to be a sign of the love of Christ and his Church: "Husbands, love your wives, as Christ loved the Church" (Eph 5:25).

Earlier in the book we saw the covenants which God made with his people. A covenant is more than a contract. A contract implies the minimal and spells out very clearly the legal responsibilities of each of the contracting parties. A covenant is an agreement between friends. It implies a loving relationship. In his covenant with us, God reaches out and loves us without restriction. We saw that his fidelity to us was absolute despite any contrary action on our part. This is why Christ was the perfect sacrament of God. His very being perfectly embodied the Father's relationship to us. Marriage then as a sacrament likewise is to be a symbol of this covenant relationship. The two parties involved are to embody that same loving relationship, that same complete, mutual self-sacrifice that Christ showed toward us.

Jesus has told us in the Gospels how complete and total this love was to be. At that time there were two rabbinic schools of thought on the question of divorce. One allowed a man to divorce his wife only for infidelity. The other allowed a man to divorce his wife for any number of reasons—including poor meals. Pharisees were constantly battling one another over the interpretation of the law of Moses. In the midst of one of these disputes, they questioned Jesus on the issue of divorce.

> Then some Pharisees came up and as a test began to ask him whether it was permissible for a husband to divorce his wife. In reply he said, "What command did Moses give you?" They answered, "Moses permitted divorce and the writing of a decree of divorce." But Jesus told them: "He wrote that commandment for you because of your stubbornness. At the beginning of creation God made them male and female; for this reason a man shall leave his father and mother and the two shall become as one. They are no longer two but one flesh. Therefore let no man separate what God has joined." Back in the house again, the disciples began to question him about this. He told them, "Whoever divorces his wife and marries another commits adultery against her; and

the woman who divorces her husband and marries another commits adultery" (Mk 10:2–12).

Jesus goes beyond the two schools of thought to forbid divorce completely. The sacrament of marriage creates an indissoluble bond between two persons because the bond between Christ and his Church is an indissoluble bond. Any marital union which does not symbolize this total and complete union of two persons is not sacramental because it is not a true symbol of that covenant between Christ and his Church. As a covenant it must be a complete commitment of the two persons. In its *Constitution on the Church in the Modern World,* Vatican II says:

> The intimate union of marriage, as a mutual giving of two persons, and the good of the children demand total fidelity from the spouses and require an unbreakable unity between them (n. 48).

In the sacrament of the Eucharist we receive the blood of the new covenant. If we understand the relationship between the sacraments of the Eucharist and matrimony, we should see clearly how they both symbolize this new covenant between God and his people. The Eucharist is a sign of the union of all in the body of Christ; matrimony is a sign of two in one flesh. The Eucharist and matrimony both reflect and make present in their actions Christ and the covenant. As Jesus said:

> "Where two or three are gathered in my name, there am I in their midst" (Mt 18:20).

The Eucharist speaks to the relation of all Christians to one another; matrimony speaks to the unique relationship of two persons. The Eucharist involves offering and sharing the body and blood of Christ; matrimony involves offering and sharing each other's body, which symbolizes their total and complete love for each other.

Marriage creates the Christian family. Husband, wife, and children are a microcosm of the Church. They are not a part of the Church; they *are* the Church. Through matrimony they become a new community of the people of God. They are a sacramental presence of Christ. The family as Church is a living sign by which we encounter the person of Christ. The deeper the couple's commitment to each other grows, the closer they are drawn to Christ, the more closely they resemble the love of Christ, and the more perfect they are as a living sacrament. The *Constitution on the Church in the Modern World* asserts:

> The Christian family springs from marriage, which is an image and a sharing in the partnership of love between Christ and the Church; it will show forth to all men Christ's living presence in the world and the authentic nature of the Church by the love and generous fruitfulness of

the spouses, by their unity and fidelity, and by the loving way in which all members of the family cooperate with each other (n. 48).

A couple's marital love can only grow through a greater sharing and communication. This takes place on different levels as they strive to know each other better and love each other deeper. The most intimate act of sharing and communication and the ultimate act of union and self-giving is the embrace of sexual intercourse. It is the strongest expression and clearest sign of who they are: two in one flesh, giving to each other completely in love. Words, gifts, and tender caresses may be signs of this love, but no other act expresses it so fully as sexual union. It is no wonder that it is called the marriage act.

Through sexual union marriage is ordered to the procreation and education of children. Children should be an outgrowth of the love of husband and wife. Sexual union is both life-giving and love-giving. To isolate the two purposes of sex is to distort its beauty and meaning. Although not every action is necessarily directed to the conception of children (e.g., intercourse during pregnancy, during infertile periods, or after menopause), the act is ordered that way nonetheless, for it still retains its openness to the transmission of life. To see the act as solely life-giving is to destroy the human aspect of sex and reduce it to a biological function. To see the act as solely love-giving is to limit the very meaning and openness of love itself. Conjugal, creative love is what specifies the marriage relationship and distinguishes it from all others. Vatican II gives us a good balance between the life and love aspects of marriage. According to the *Constitution on the Church in the Modern World:*

> The divine law throws light on the meaning of married love, protects it and leads it to truly human fulfillment. Whenever Christian spouses in a spirit of sacrifice and trust in divine providence carry out their duties of procreation with generous human and Christian responsibility, they glorify the Creator and perfect themselves in Christ. . . .
>
> But marriage is not merely for the procreation of children: its nature as an indissoluble compact between two people and the good of the children demand that the mutual love of the partners be properly shown, and that it should grow and mature. Even in cases where despite the intense desire of the spouses there are no children, marriage still retains its character of being a whole manner and communion of life and preserves its value and indissolubility (n. 50).

As these words are read, many may understandably comment that these are just words: very idealistic but far from the reality. After all, are there not many marriages that end in divorce? Look at all the existing marriages that are tragedies. Often the most bitter hatred has grown out of the marriage of two people. The ideal presented in the sacrament of matrimony is often far from the reality. This seems to call into question the whole idea of marriage as a sacrament.

However, this same thing can be said about sacraments in general. Christ was the only perfect sacrament. Even the Church is a flawed symbol of the ideal. Until the second coming of Christ we will always have imperfect models. Not everyone who is baptized and confirmed becomes the model Christian. But we still look at the more successful ones to give us an idea of the perfect model. And so it is with marriage.

The news commentator Paul Harvey often gives the names of different couples around the country who are celebrating their sixtieth or seventieth wedding anniversary. These people stand as inspirations to others who are struggling to develop their marriage relationship. Why have they lasted together so long? It is not because the two had the same interests. Nor is it because there was perfect compatibility. They simply loved each other and were giving of themselves completely to deepen that love. Things were not always easy. There were moments of animosity and even indifference as well as moments of joy and ecstasy. But through all of this there was a growth taking place. A love began. A commitment to each other was made because of this love. Their love was deepening. The sacrament of matrimony was living in them. Day by day, year by year, they were symbolizing more clearly that love covenant between Christ and us, his people, the Church.

QUESTIONS FOR REFLECTION

1. Review the distinction between contract and covenant. Examining your own marriage or the marriage of someone you know, cite examples of how marriage is a contract rather than a covenant._____

2. There is a communal dimension to every sacrament. How do you see that exemplified in the sacrament of marriage?_____

3. How in concrete ways do you see marriage as the sign of Christ and his Church?_____

HOLY ORDERS

When the thirteen colonies broke away from England and won their independence after many years of fighting, they were able to unite under the leadership of General George Washington. He had such qualities that he emerged as the natural leader. Often movements receive their vitality from a very charismatic leader who gives vision and direction. But all human beings are mortal. The key to the survival of any movement is how it deals with the question of leadership. If the movement is able to create a leadership position independent of a particular person, then the movement can survive. Because the thirteen colonies eventually agreed on a Constitution that resolved the leadership question, an orderly transition took place when George Washington stepped down and the new president, John Adams, assumed authority. There was truly a permanent government and nation of the United States of America.

Jesus also was a charismatic leader. But like any human being his time on earth was limited. So in order to enable his mission to continue beyond his death, he too had to resolve the leadership question. He chose certain of his followers to assume the leadership role. The original group to assume this role was known as the Twelve. The number had a special significance because of the twelve tribes of Israel. A larger group than the Twelve, but not exclusive of it either, were the apostles. The apostles included all those who had seen the risen Jesus and were personally commissioned by him to proclaim the Gospel. The apostles were the key to the spread of the early Church after Pentecost.

As the Church grew through the ages, its structure changed, but the key to its continuity is that its leadership can be traced to the apostles. We say that the Church is apostolic in its origin. Its leaders are seen as commissioned to carry on the work of Christ. Unlike secular leadership, Church leadership is seen in terms of love, not power. The true leader of the Church is Christ, and anyone commissioned by Christ is called to enable a community of love to exist. If the Church is no longer a community of love, it has lost its identity. The essence of leadership in the Church consists in proclaiming the Gospel of Christ and administering the sacraments. A leader of the Church then functions in ministering to his community in this way.

The Church took a number of years before properly defining its leadership. The original term used for its leader was *episcopos,* overseer. The word used from the post-apostolic age to today is bishop. And the sacrament through which a man receives this commission to leadership is called holy orders. The local church is called a diocese. And there is only one person possessing this leadership role in each local church.

It may be appropriate to mention that the Pope is ordained to leadership because he is ordained bishop. He is primarily the bishop of Rome. It is only because he is the bishop of Rome that he is the leader of the universal Church. His primacy stems from the fact that Peter was commissioned by Jesus to be the leader among the apostles. As the apostolic Church became more settled, Peter assumed the leadership of the Church at Rome. After Peter's death the leadership of the universal Church has been passed on to his successors in Rome.

As the Christian community grew in number, it was apparent that the Twelve could not assume all the leadership responsibilities by themselves. Therefore the Seven were appointed to take care of temporal affairs like food distribution and care of the widows, in order that the Twelve might be free to proclaim the Word. Later some of the Seven also preached and baptized. Their successors in the Church of today are the deacons. Later on we see that there developed in local communities to aid the *episcopoi* a group of men called *presbyteroi,* presbyters or elders. Although the distinction was not so clear, their successors in the Church of today are the priests. The term "priest," however, is not used in this sense in the New Testament. It is only used in reference to Jesus Christ, the eternal high priest (Hebrews), and to our sharing through baptism in the priesthood of Christ (1 Peter 3).

The only person who receives all of the sacrament of holy orders is the bishop. However, he has delegated some of his leadership responsibilities to two other groups of men in his local church: the priests and the deacons. They each share in their own way in the sacrament of holy orders by the authority of their bishop.

A priest is given that title because of his leadership in the eucharistic celebration. He alone has been ordained by his bishop to preside at the altar and to offer with the believing community in the name of Jesus Christ, the high priest, the gift of Jesus Christ, the victim. From this presidential role comes his authority to preside at the celebration of the sacraments of penance and anointing of the sick. He has been commissioned to initiate people into the Church through baptism and, at times, confirmation, to witness marriages, and to preach the good news of salvation.

Diakonia means ministry, or service, and a deacon has been commissioned to be of special service to the believing community. Like St. Stephen, the first martyr, the deacon has been commissioned to preach the good news and baptize people into the Church. But his ordained leadership consists principally in service to the believing community. Although the diaconate as a permanent office antedates the priesthood, it had fallen into disuse and was only functioning as a step to the priesthood. However, the Second Vatican Council called for the restoration of the permanent diaconate.

Under the Church's current discipline, no man may be ordained either a priest or a bishop unless he is unmarried. No man, once he has received the sacrament of holy orders, whether as a bishop, priest, or deacon, may marry. This unmarried state chosen for the sake of service to the Church is known as celibacy. It does not pertain to the essence of holy orders. Married men, in fact, may be ordained deacons in the Western rite, and in the Eastern rite they may also be ordained priests. But for a number of historical, theological, and pastoral reasons, celibacy has been the practice in the Latin or Western rite for hundreds of years.

For most of us the person whom we encounter most often as the ordained spiritual leader is our parish priest. Our own parish is in reality the Church, and the priest is commissioned by the bishop to lead that local community of faith. Since a Christian sees leadership in a different way than secular society does, the leadership function of the priest is related not to ruling but to service. The priest exercises his leadership by (1) proclaiming the Word of God, (2) presiding at worship, (3) serving the Christian community, and (4) serving mankind. (For a deeper insight into the life and ministry of the priest, see *As One Who Serves: Reflections on the Pastoral Ministry on Priests in the United States,* United States Catholic Conference, 1977.)

1. *Proclaiming the Word of God.* In the *Decree on the Ministry and Life of Priests,* Vatican II says:

> The people of God is formed into one in the first place by the Word of the living God, which is quite rightly sought from the mouth of the priest. For since nobody can be saved who has not first believed, it is the first task of priests as co-workers of the bishops to preach the Gospel to all men (n. 4).

The power of God's Word cannot be overemphasized. It is only when people become nourished by the Word that they are impelled to approach the sacraments. As was seen earlier, every sacramental celebration involves proclaiming the Word. With the reforms of Vatican II, preaching is a part of the life of the priest more than ever before. To be familiar with the Scriptures through study and prayer is essential. Although not ordained, catechists also share in this preaching ministry, for proclaiming God's Word also includes evangelization, catechesis, speaking out on contemporary problems, and witnessing to the world as persons of faith.

2. *Presiding at Worship.* So often the life of a parish can be perceived by how that community worships. People in today's mobile society often are willing to travel many miles to a parish because that parish has a dynamic liturgy. This depends on how the priest is exercising his leadership, how he presides at worship. A priest may be a mediocre preacher and be careless in ritual but have an effective presidential style. He may recognize the gifts of different people in his community: lectors, cantors, commentators, artists, musicians. Because he has enabled these gifts to be utilized effectively in the Mass and other liturgical celebrations, the parish is alive. People participate and respond enthusiastically. The priest has presided well at worship. He has shown himself to be a gifted leader.

3. *Serving the Christian Community.* Jesus said: "I am in your midst as the one who serves you" (Lk 22:27). To be of service to one's community is to follow the example of our leader Jesus. As the priest brings Christ into the community through Word and sacrament, his pastoral ministry brings Christ to his community in a different way. When John the Baptist was in prison, he wanted evidence that Jesus was truly the leader long awaited. Jesus' answer was addressed in terms of his ministry to his people:

> "Go back and report to John what you hear and see: the blind recover their sight, cripples walk, lepers are cured, the deaf hear, dead men are raised to life, and the poor have the good news preached to them" (Mt 11:4–5).

The priest in service of the community settles quarrels, comforts the suffering, visits the sick and dying, often even healing them, and gives hope to the depressed. His service also involves organizing the parish, promoting leadership among his community, and supporting the various communities within his parish (catechetical community, marriage encounter, cursillo, charismatic groups, base communities).

4. *Serving Mankind.* A priest can be so immersed in his own parish ministry that he can ignore the world about him. As a leader he needs to be aware of the larger community about him. It is his responsibility to see that his parish community is looking outward as well as inward. A Church with a vibrant faith life within should also be one with a thirst for social justice without.

Like all sacraments holy orders is a sacrament of the community for the community. The bishop, deacon, and priest are called from the community by the community to lead through service to the community. Who ordains? The bishop. But he ordains in the name of the community. A person cannot lead without a group willing to follow, cannot preach without an audience, cannot celebrate without a worshiping community. It is in reality the Church, the people of God, which really makes the leader. Holy orders is the action of the entire body of Christ.

QUESTIONS FOR REFLECTION

1. In what way are you able to see the priest as minister to the community?

2. How do you see leadership in relationship to the sacrament of holy orders?

3. What are the Christ-like qualities specific to the deacon? to the priest? to the bishop? What are the ones that pertain to all of us?

4. Can you see any relationship between the communal nature of the sacrament of holy orders and the aspect of a call by the Church community?

UNIT SIX

GOD'S CALL: OUR RESPONSE

1. GRACE: THE PRESENCE OF GOD

There is an orphanage a few miles north of the city of Ensenada, Mexico. It is sponsored by a confederation of Churches of Christ from the United States. One particular American felt especially called to serve these orphans. Being a bachelor Bill was able to spend much of his money and virtually all of his spare time working at the orphanage. He was constantly transporting there all the food and clothing he could get, spent back-breaking hours digging ditches in order to lay pipes so that there might be running water in the place, and helped lay bricks, paint buildings, and clear ground. Above all, he loved to spend time with the children. He played with the younger ones and taught some of the older boys practical skills.

One particular boy, José Antonio, caught his attention. It was not because he was the most lovable. In fact, the contrary was closer to the truth. The boy was an absolute terror. He fought with everyone, often stole whatever was left unwatched, and seemed totally disinterested in doing anything constructive. His dress was sloppy, and he had such an aversion to bathing that it was odious even to go near him. He was mean and ungrateful, and obscenities were so much a part of his speech that he hardly was aware of it.

For some reason Bill loved José and really wanted to help the boy, but every effort he made to reach José ended in failure. He tried to play basketball with him, to take him to the beach, and to teach him how to read better, but José just did not want to open up. Perhaps he had been so hurt when his parents abandoned him that he felt it was not even worth trying again. Or perhaps he never even knew what it was to be loved and to love in return.

Gradually José was drawn to Bill. It was not so much what Bill did for him as his persistence in staying present to him. Then one day José broke down and cried in Bill's arms. The boy suddenly realized how much Bill meant to him. He was able to let go of himself and be vulnerable to another. To find someone who really loved him and whom he could love in return gave him a whole new orientation in his life. José was able to look out from himself and discover relationships with others.

The boy was not an instant angel. He still fought with people, and his language still was peppered with obscenities, but he was trying. With Bill around to goad him on and to pick him up when he failed, he gradually was transformed. Legal problems prevented Bill from adopting José, but in virtually every other way the two were like father and son. Through their loving relationship José looked at the world with different eyes. He saw a world of beauty, of generosity, and of love instead of a world of ugliness, self-centeredness, and hatred. All this happened because a man reached out and touched him, loved him and remained present until he was able to respond in love.

This is a beautiful story, but a similar story and an even more beautiful one is that of God with us. What we have seen so many times in this book and what the Scriptures are constantly telling us is that God always takes the initiative. He is the one who is present, the one who, despite our faults, never abandons us. When Israel because of her sins was reduced to nothing as a captive people in Babylon, it was God who assured his presence and fidelity:

> Can a mother forget her infant, be without tenderness for the child of
> her womb? Even should she forget, I will never forget you (Is 49:15).

Jesus is the living sign of God's commitment to us. God became present in the flesh.

What God is trying to tell us is how much he loves each and every one of us. He wants to turn us away from a sterile, useless life and experience *real* love: the love which he offers us. As he began his public ministry, Jesus said: "This is the time of fulfillment. The reign of God is at hand. Reform your lives and believe in the Gospel" (Mk 1:15). That message is the Gospel or good news. John expressed the good news in a slightly different way than Jesus, but his message is essentially the same: "God is Love" (1 Jn 4:8). The extent of God's love toward us is described by John:

> God's love was revealed in our midst in this way: he sent his only Son
> into the world that we might have life through him. Love, then, consists
> in this: not that we have loved God but that he has loved us and has
> sent his Son as an offering for our sins (1 Jn 4:9–10).

The whole love relationship of God and us is most familiarly known as "grace." Too often God's grace is thought of as meaning gifts in the sense of things: wealth, fortune, health, strong virtue, wisdom, or spiritual energy. But grace is not a private possession which one has. What John is telling us and what all Scripture tells us is that primarily grace means the favor by which God gives himself. He is present to us and wishes us to be present to him. Keeping in mind the story of Bill and José may help us appreciate the whole dynamism of the grace of God.

Before we were even aware of anything, God loved us. Our very existence is the result of God's love for us. While we still lived a life of sin, God loved us. He was present to us. He was trying to draw us to himself. Even before we were willing to respond to God's love, he was present. It was the presence of Jesus in the world that enabled God to be present to us. God's very presence in wanting us to love him is an attractive power. There is no force. For love to be true, it must be a free decision on our part.

Jesus says: "No one can come to me unless the Father who sent me draws him" (Jn 6:44). God must draw us, or attract us, before we can even begin to respond. This action is so real, so intimate, that God is writing it in our hearts. It is an inner guidance coming directly from God. Jeremiah the prophet says:

> I will place my law within them, and write it upon their hearts; I will be their God, and they shall be my people. No longer will they have need to teach their friends and kinsmen how to know the Lord. All, from the least to greatest, shall know me (Jer 31:33–34).

The prophet Hosea even uses the word "lure." It is like the spouse luring his or her mate to make love. This is what God first does to us. Augustine once said: "You have made us for yourself, O Lord, and our hearts will not rest until they rest in you." There is deeply imbedded in each of us a desire for the good, a longing for the transcendent, a remote crying out for God. Even the most committed atheist, even the most vicious of people, has this. Why? God wants all of us to be saved and be part of his family, and, therefore, he is present drawing them to himself. God's presence enables us to come to that point where from the core of our being we can freely say "Abba," Father, and enter into that new relationship of love. As Paul says:

> All who are led by the Spirit of God are sons of God. You did not receive a spirit of slavery leading you back into fear, but a spirit of adoption through which we cry out, "Abba!" (that is, "Father") (Rom 8:14–15).

To appreciate Paul's idea of grace, read slowly Romans 8.

Once people have accepted God's initiative and made a free option to love God, they are living the life of grace. Such people are said to be in the state of grace. Since this life is a *living* presence of God, it is something that is just beginning. José was not an instant angel once he responded to Bill's love, but his whole orientation had changed. He was moving in the right direction. The more we make decisions based on that basic one to respond to God's love, the more deeply we live God's life. It has grown out of that inner attraction which God originally offered us. Sanctifying grace is not some *thing;* rather it means that we are freely living as accepted children of God. We are children of God because we love God and our neighbor. We have a love commitment to others and to God.

A term often used in the past, "habitual grace," can be misleading. It could be more accurately described as the effect of grace. Grace is not a possession. Bonaventure once said: "To have is to be had." To have grace would mean to have God. It is not that we possess God; it is more that we are possessed by God. And that is someone whom no one can remove from us. As Paul says:

> Who will separate us from the love of Christ? Trial, or distress, or persecution, or hunger, or nakedness, or danger, or the sword? As Scripture says: "For your sake we are being slain all the day long; we are looked upon as sheep to be slaughtered." Yet in all this we are more than conquerors because of him who has loved us. For I am certain that neither death nor life, neither angels nor principalities, neither the present nor the future, nor powers, neither height nor depth nor any other creature, will be able to separate us from the love of God that comes to us in Christ Jesus, our Lord (Rom 8:35–39).

A word to be used interchangeably with grace is "favor." To do a favor is not to put a person in debt but to show one's friendship or love. Bill did José a favor. It was so great a favor that it changed his life. Bill's favor of loving presence and faithful commitment to José only gradually enabled him to enter this love relationship. But the favor was *not* a thing. Neither is God's favor. His favor or grace is this living and loving presence of God himself in us, in the Church, and in the world.

QUESTIONS FOR REFLECTION

1. How have you seen God work in your own life? Be specific.

2. In what ways have you experienced God as an attracting force almost begging you to love him?

3. Identify people whose very lives have been occasions to enable others to experience God's presence.

4. How might you as a catechist enable others to experience this presence of God?

2. LIFE OF GRACE: ACCEPTANCE OR REJECTION

In the last section on grace we saw that it is the living and loving presence of God. The emphasis was on God's initiative. It is an invitation on God's part. He is calling us to share in his life. God's presence is offered, not imposed. God wants us to love him, but he does not demand it. The life of grace in us lies at the root of our freedom. Although grace is always offered, whether we accept it or not is our free decision. Our emphasis in this chapter will be on grace as accepted.

The clearest ideas of God's invitation are found in the life of Jesus. His first invitations were to his closest disciples, the Twelve. One of them, Matthew, was a tax-collector, one of the most despicable jobs in Jewish society. It was, however, quite lucrative. Yet at Jesus' invitation Matthew followed Jesus (see Mt 9:9ff). His whole life was changed. Another tax-collector, Zacchaeus, also was called by Jesus to live a new kind of life. In accepting God's life of grace, Zacchaeus asserted:

"I give half my belongings, Lord, to the poor. If I have defrauded anyone in the least, I pay him back fourfold" (Lk 19:8).

On the other hand, we have the story of a rich man who was offered the new life of grace but was not able to respond because of his attachment to wealth:

One of the ruling class asked him then, "Good teacher, what must I do to share in everlasting life?" Jesus said to him, "Why call me 'good'?

None is good but God alone. You know the commandments: You shall not commit adultery. You shall not kill. You shall not steal. You shall not bear dishonest witness. Honor your father and your mother."

He replied, "I have kept all these since I was a boy." When Jesus heard this he said to him: "There is one thing further you must do. Sell all you have and give to the poor. You will have treasure in heaven. Then come and follow me." On hearing this he grew melancholy, for he was a very rich man. When Jesus observed this he said: "How hard it will be for the rich to go into the kingdom of God! Indeed, it is easier for a camel to go through a needle's eye than for a rich man to enter the kingdom of heaven" (Lk 18:18–25).

We have then two responses to God's initiative of love: acceptance or rejection. One is the life of grace; the other is the life of sin. The free response to love God is the moment of conversion. We have made a decision to live a Christ-centered life. Once our basic orientation is made, all our other actions flow from it. Matthew made that basic move to follow Christ. Because of that he left his tax-collector's post, traveled around with Jesus, and even eventually helped spread the good news about Jesus after he died. Zacchaeus made that basic move to follow Christ. Because of that he received Jesus into his home and reaffirmed his custom of giving half his riches to the poor and repaying fourfold anyone he had cheated. The spirit in which they lived, the basic orientation of their life, was more important than the actual activity. It was the mentality behind it that gave value to their actual activity. This basic origin of their whole life is often called the fundamental option. Fr. Bernard Haring, a well-known moral theologian, says:

> Conversion involves the whole human being in all his fundamental relations. It is total response to God's call, a fundamental decision.... The fundamental option, if it is a mature option for God and good, is the road to wholeness. A conversion to the Gospel in living faith is much more than acceptance of a complete code of morality. It is a rebirth to new life, to fullness of life in Christ Jesus; it is insertion into the stream of his love for all humankind and union with his love for the Father (*Free and Faithful in Christ*, Vol. 1, New York: The Seabury Press, 1978, p. 419).

The rich young man was given the same offer as Matthew and Zacchaeus, but he was too self-centered. He was too attached to his wealth and possessions. Grace was offered; grace was rejected. Where the fundamental option to God is the life of grace, the rejection of that life is sin. Did the young man choose to live in sin? Maybe not. But he certainly rejected an opportunity to grow more deeply in the life of God. His attitude was to remain self-centered and to cling to his possessions. Every activity that followed was significantly different than if he had been able to let go completely and follow Christ, for it stemmed from a different orientation to life. It was self-centered rather than God-centered.

Without the existence of God's invitation, a fundamental option would not be possible. In fact, if we did not know of this new life of grace, we would feel that a self-centered life is just part of human nature. It is precisely because of the redeeming grace of Jesus Christ that we know of the reality of original sin. We as humans share in the solidarity of sin. "Through one man sin entered the world and with sin death, death thus coming to all men inasmuch as all sinned" (Rom 5:12). However, because Jesus came to the world, God is able to offer us this new life of grace, the ability to live a totally God-centered life. "But despite the increase of sin, grace has far surpassed it" (Rom 5:20).

Too much we have seen original sin as a blotch on the soul which was passed down through human generation. This view has caused us to view even the tiny infant as sin-filled and does not make sense. On the other hand, to deny the existence of original sin would not only be a heresy; it would be foolish. In our age where totalitarian dictatorships abound, where religion is persecuted, where mass executions and genocide have occurred, where nuclear weapons are stockpiled capable of obliterating hundreds of millions of human beings, and where the wealthy few can accumulate and hoard vast holdings of land and food while their neighbors are starving, the existence of original sin can hardly be denied. These evils are the effects of mankind's tendency to live self-directed, egocentric lives. This is what original sin is about. This tendency may only be overcome by the redeeming grace of Christ.

St. Peter made his fundamental option to God when he left his fishing boat and traveled with the man from Galilee. Yet he had not completely overcome his evil tendency. He had his setbacks, was not totally into a deep prayer life, and still had a violent streak in him. He even at one point denied Jesus three times. But despite his imperfection, Peter's basic orientation was God-centered. He was living the life of grace. His sins did not destroy that life.

Because of that inherent tendency to evil, our lives are not perfect. Even after we have accepted the life of grace, we still sin. This does not necessarily destroy our love relationship with God. Sin may hinder our growth and damage our Christ-centered orientation. But mortal sin alone destroys the life of grace. Mortal sin means a complete rejection of God's law of love and destruction of that fundamental option. Grave actions contrary to God's laws are not mortal sins; they are really the effects of mortal sin. For example, what makes murder or adultery a mortal sin is not the action in itself but the inner attitude that enabled the person to perform the act. It is an external sign of our rejection of a Christ-centered life in favor of an egocentric one. Because of the radical nature of both grace and mortal sin, one does not fluctuate between the two on a regular basis.

The ultimate evil of mortal sin is everlasting punishment in hell. It is not so much that God has sent us there but that we have chosen it. If our final decision in this life were to reject God, we would simply be living out that life which we so freely chose. God's offer of love is free. The existence of hell is an affirmation that God has allowed us the freedom to accept as well as reject him.

Christ's offer of grace, love, and divine life is one that is always present. The fundamental option is our acceptance of Christ's offer. We could also call it sanctifying grace. The final option in our lives is the everlasting life of heaven. Heaven then is the everlasting ratification of our option to live the life of Christ. St. Paul says:

> Now that you are freed from sin and have become slaves of God, your benefit is sanctification as you tend toward eternal life. The wages of sin is death, but the gift of God is eternal life in Christ Jesus our Lord (Rom 6:22–23).

God is the ultimate source of grace, but often we, his people, are the human instruments through whom he makes himself present. It is ordinary people we encounter each day who enable us to make our fundamental option and live the life of God. Catherine de Hueck Doherty cites a beautiful story of how that happened to one young girl.

> The girl was a prostitute; she never denied it. In fact, she seemed to flaunt it. She would loudly demand to be served ahead of the long and patient line of people waiting for clothing because, she said, she was tired of "standing too long after her night's work!"
> Of course, she didn't get that attention, for justice to others had to be guarded and priorities observed. So she would curse, in a steady, droning monotone for over an hour or more, until her turn finally came to examine the clothes we had and to select the things she needed. Somehow the obscene words sounded strange coming from her, for she was young and beautiful. Admittedly, it sounded as though she had had a lot of practice!
> Often the line of patiently waiting people would shuffle uneasily under the impact of her profane deluge of words. Often, too, passersby would hurl insults back at her. But she simply went on cursing, oblivious to the waiting line, the city, oblivious to everything but her desire to get to the head of that line.
> At long last her turn would come and she would step through the door of our clothing center, a storefront which opened into a busy slum street. The worker in charge was a young and beautiful girl. She had to listen to this stream of filth for over an hour every day of the week—except Sunday! She bore it patiently.
> Funny, how serene that worker's face was, how gentle and understanding she always appeared. Every day she would suggest a cup of coffee to the girl to help take the coarseness out of her throat. Always the girl drank the coffee and then, very critically, looked over the secondhand clothing we had to give away until she found what she wanted.
> Three hundred and sixty-five days in a year, minus Sundays and holidays. That gave our workers about 300 days to listen to abuse, make coffee and give out a dress to this girl. That's a lot of hours, a lot of days, a lot of abuse, a lot of coffee and a lot of love!
> Then one day the prostitute was sober, quiet, watchful and even

a little timid. She knocked politely and entered when bade. Then, standing straight and tall, she looked into the staff worker's beautiful face and asked point-blank why she had been so patient. Why hadn't she called the cops? Why had she so sweetly endured insults and injuries? Why had she given her the coffee, the dresses, the polite and gentle service? Why had she never complained?

Having spent herself with questions, she stood quite rigid, as if bracing herself for an answer she was afraid to hear.

All the worker said was, "Oh, that's very simple. *I love you.*" The prostitute swayed as if struck in the face, and out of her very soul came the cry, "Me! Why?"

Even gentler than before came the reply: "Because you are Christ to me, because he died for love of both of us, because I am your sister in him, because I am here to love and serve you."

The girl crumpled to the floor. She wept with deep, heavy sobs that slowly subsided, leaving her spent and quiet. Slowly she got up. She said: "I never heard such things, but I know you mean business because . . . because you were always the same. There was always the coffee, the dresses . . . yes, now I know. I want to love as you do. Teach me how."

The girl was a prostitute. She never hid it. She flaunted it. But after that day she took instructions. She was eventually baptized and went to confession and received Communion. Today, in that big city, there are 17 of them that I know of, prostitutes who wept at the feet of Christ. They all arose, cleansed and whole, and it was this girl who had brought them to him. (*Not Without Parables,* Notre Dame: Ave Maria Press, 1977, pp. 69–71).

Where did God's grace operate for the prostitute? Before she even thought of changing her attitude and ways, God was present offering his love. The girl was not originally living the life of grace not because God was not offering it but because she was not accepting it. The young girl working at the clothing center became an instrument of God's grace. Because this girl was so full of God's love, the prostitute began to encounter God's presence through her. When the girl told the prostitute that she loved her, the prostitute began to experience the love of God. She suddenly began to change her life. She had accepted God's grace. She made that fundamental option for a God-centered life. Conversion had taken place. The instructions and sacraments that followed were an effect of that conversion.

Maybe we cannot point to an event in our lives which marked our conversion. The life of grace may have been so deeply ingrained in our family that our lives were always Christ-centered. But for many of us it has happened. It is not unusual for our young people to have a period of time in their lives when they reject all the religious training of their childhood. Such a period is often necessary to prepare them for that conversion moment. Then their faith is really their own. They have accepted out of complete freedom the love of God because they wanted it. It was their fundamental option.

QUESTIONS FOR REFLECTION

1. At what moment in your life did you make your fundamental option for God? What events led up to it?

2. What obstacles might we run into which deafen our ears to God's call to conversion?

3. In looking at sin in terms of relationship rather than law breaking, why would such a view reflect more clearly the Gospel call to conversion?

4. Describe in terms of events you encounter each day the reality of original sin.

5. In light of that, how do you see Jesus as the "lamb of God who takes away the sin of the world"?

3. MORALITY

One of the most shameful phases of American history was the tolerance of the institution of slavery. Tens of thousands of Africans were forcibly captured, locked in chains, shipped thousands of miles to our shores, and sold to the highest bidder. The slave and all his or her descendants were the legal property of their owner unless they were sold to another.

The main work of slaves was picking cotton. They worked from dawn to dusk performing this back-breaking chore. The slaves were totally subservient to their masters. They had to obey them in all things. To assure compliance, the master saw that punishment was swift and sure. The whip was the common instrument, and even death was not considered an unreasonable penalty. The slaves did what was right to save their own skin. Without whips and chains they would have done no work. There was no other motivation than fear of punishment.

Were we to judge what was right or wrong by our chances of punishment and reward, we would have a very low sense of morality. If fear of punishment were the only basis for Christian morality, our moral values would be little different from that of slaves. If we view the Christian code of morality as nothing more than a list of do's and don'ts, we are really distorting both the Scriptures and the law of Christ.

The context for the Jewish sense of morality begins with the covenant. It is the enduring sign of God's relationship with his people, Israel. Jewish law was seen as a consequence of covenant. This is exemplified in the shema:

Hear, O Israel! The Lord is our God, the Lord alone! Therefore, you shall love the Lord our God, with all your heart, and with all your soul, and with all your strength (Dt 6:4–5).

The first part of the passage expresses this special relationship of Israel and God. And the second part states what Israel's response to this is to be. Living out the law was a sign of Israel's intimacy with God.

The law was not seen as some burdensome obligation but rather as evidence of Israel's special call by God to be his own. It was something about which Israel could be proud, for it separated her from all other nations. Observing the law was seen as a source of joy. Psalm 119 is a wonderful expression of this joy:

Happy are they whose way is blameless,
    who walk in the law of the Lord.
Happy are they who observe his decrees
    who seek him with all their heart (vv. 1–3).
With all my heart I seek you;
    let me not stray from your commands (v. 10).
In your statutes I will delight;
    I will not forget your word (v. 16).

> The law of your mouth is to me more precious
> than thousands of gold and silver pieces (v. 72).

It is in light of this view of the law that we must view the ten commandments or decalogue. They are not, strictly speaking, a code of morality. The list is primarily a religious document, not a moral one. It begins, like the shema, with a statement of the unique relationship of Israel and God:

> I, the Lord, am your God, who brought you out of the land of Egypt, that place of slavery (Ex 20:2).

Then the document goes on to state how Israel is to respond:

> "You shall not have other gods besides me. You shall not carve idols for yourselves in the shape of anything in the sky above or on the earth below or in the waters beneath the earth; you shall not bow down before them or worship them. For I, the Lord, your God, am a jealous God, inflicting punishment for their fathers' wickedness on the children of those who hate me, down to the third and fourth generation; but bestowing mercy down to the thousandth generation, on the children of those who love me and keep my commandments.
> "You shall not take the name of the Lord, your God, in vain. For the Lord will not leave unpunished him who takes his name in vain.
> "Remember to keep holy the sabbath day. Six days you may labor and do all your work, but the seventh day is the sabbath of the Lord, your God. No work may be done then either by you, or your son or daughter, or your male or female slave, or your beast, or by the alien who lives with you. In six days the Lord made the heavens and the earth, the sea and all that is in them; but on the seventh day he rested. That is why the Lord has blessed the sabbath day and made it holy.
> "Honor your father and your mother, that you may have a long life in the land which the Lord, your God, is giving you.
> "You shall not kill.
> "You shall not commit adultery.
> "You shall not steal.
> "You shall not bear false witness against your neighbor.
> "You shall not covet your neighbor's wife, nor his male or female slave, nor his ox or ass, nor anything else that belongs to him" (Ex 20:3–17).

The motivation for keeping these commands is that Israel may maintain her unique relationship with God. These commands never were intended to be a complete moral code. They are characterized more from what they leave out than from what they include. You shall not kill your neighbor, but you can eliminate the foreigner. You shall not commit adultery, but there are other forms of sexual actions. This is not to fault the decalogue. A complete code of morality simply was not its intent.

It was not even primarily interested in the individual but the community. The prime concern of Israel was her own existence as a people chosen by God. Therefore, the concern of Israel was about sin insofar as it affected the community. An idolatrous nation was severing the intimate relationship with God. Actions which undermined the community threatened the existence of Israel itself. Without Israel there was no covenant. That is why the decalogue was primarily a religious rather than a moral code.

Our morality as Christians is rooted in Jesus. Like the law of the Israelites, the law of Christ is based on a response to the love which God has already initiated toward us. Jesus says:

> As the Father has loved me,
> so I have loved you.
> Live on in my love.
> You will live in my love
> if you keep my commandments,
> even as I have kept my Father's commandments,
> and live in his love (Jn 15:9–10).

Love becomes the foundation of our morality. As the Father has loved Jesus, Jesus has loved us. In response we are to live in that love. We live in that love by loving one another.

> This is my commandment: love one another as I have loved you (Jn 15:12).

Jesus summarized his moral teaching in the Gospels through the two great commandments: love of God and love of neighbor. The Gospel accounts of Matthew, Mark, and Luke all relate the story. In Mark's Gospel a scribe came up and asked Jesus' opinion about which is the first of the commandments. Since the rabbis listed 713 of them, Jesus had a lot to choose from.

> Jesus replied: "This is the first:
>   'Hear, O Israel! The Lord our God is Lord alone!
>   Therefore you shall love the Lord your God
>   with all your heart,
>   with all your soul,
>   with all your mind,
>   and with all your strength.'
> This is the second,
>   'You shall love your neighbor as yourself.'
> There is no other commandment greater than these" (Mk 12:29–31).

Jesus has not given us anything new with the two great commandments. Both are found in the Old Testament (Dt 6:5; Lv 19:18). What he has done is to take these two commandments and bring them together so that his followers might see the close relationship between love of God and love of neighbor. Luke's Gospel extends the idea further when Jesus redefines "neighbor" to mean not merely another Israelite but anyone whom we encounter, even the Samaritan (see Lk 11:29–45, the story of the good Samaritan). St. Paul continues this line of thought when he says:

> Owe no debt to anyone except the debt that binds us to love one another. He who loves his neighbor has fulfilled the law. The commandments . . . are all summed up in this: "You shall love your neighbor as yourself." Love never wrongs the neighbor; hence love is the fulfillment of the law (Rom 13:8–10).

The two great commandments become the motivating force for Jesus' moral teaching.

What Jesus wants in us is not a slave morality but a love morality.

> I no longer speak of you as slaves,
> for a slave does not know what his master is about.
> Instead, I call you friends,
> since I have made known to you all that I heard from my Father (Jn 15:15).

In a slave morality it is: "Do it or else." But Jesus simply said: "If you love me, keep my commandments." There are no threats of impending doom, no curses. Most of the things two people in love do for each other are out of love, not force. If a sense of obligation were the only thing holding a marriage together, that marriage would be a shaky one. If our sense of legal obligation is the only thing impelling us to lead a moral life, our relationship with God would be a shaky one.

Matthew's Gospel presents Jesus as the new Moses, the new lawgiver. The body of the Gospel is divided into five books, just like the Pentateuch. As Moses went to Mount Sinai to receive the decalogue, Jesus goes to a mountain to preach his law on the Sermon on the Mount. The sermon begins with the blueprint for happiness in following his law, the beatitudes:

> When he saw the crowds he went up on the mountainside. After he had sat down his disciples gathered around him, and he began to teach them:
> "How blest are the poor in spirit: the reign of God is theirs.
> Blest too are the sorrowing; they shall be consoled.
> Blest are the lowly; they shall inherit the land.
> Blest are they who hunger and thirst for holiness: they shall have their fill.
> Blest are they who show mercy; mercy shall be theirs.

Blest are the single-hearted for they shall see God.

Blest too the peacemakers; they shall be called sons of God.

Blest are those persecuted for holiness' sake; the reign of God is theirs" (Mt 5:1–10).

The first beatitude typifies the attitude of mind upon which the other beatitudes are based: a humility and poverty of spirit. They are blest because they know they need God. It is when we live our lives motivated by the desire to follow God's will and live his way of life that we find happiness. Jesus is the first of the poor in spirit who, through the Holy Spirit, acknowledged everything as a gift from his Father and lived a life of service to his brothers and sisters without seeking anything in return.

In the sermon Jesus insists that he has not come to abolish the law but to perfect it. He was saying that perfecting the law means going beyond a minimalism. Don't just avoid murder; avoid any kind of anger. If someone is upset with you, go out of your way to be reconciled with that person. Don't just avoid adultery; don't even think lustfully. Forget about an eye for an eye; turn the other cheek. If someone wants your shirt, give your coat as well. Don't just love your friends; love your enemies. And so Jesus continues with other aspects of the law.

With Jesus it is not so much a question of what I have to do or what I have to avoid. Rather, Jesus calls us to respond generously and wholeheartedly to love of God and neighbor. The questions we ask ourselves and the answers we reach are much deeper than that of obeying or disobeying a law. Our whole attitude of moral living becomes person-centered rather than law-centered.

In the section of grace we saw that when we have received God's initiative of love totally, that response is a fundamental option to live out the life of God. Our day-to-day decisions of what to do and what not to do are the result of that basic attitude of drawing closer to God. When we are confronted with a moral choice, our question should be: "Is this bringing me closer to God or not? Am I doing this out of selfish motivation or am I really concerned about the needs of others?" Two persons may perform the same action. The morality of that action comes from the person's own attitude and motivation, rather than simply from the deed.

For example, John Millette owns a canning factory. His friend, Harry O'Dowd, is in the same business. In a sense, they are competitors with each other, but the demand is large enough so that neither company profits at the other's expense. The union is trying to organize the workers in the two companies. Although John is not too excited about negotiating with a union, he also realizes that his employees may personally feel more secure with a union if they are unionized. And so he is willing to have an election and abide by the decision. Harry, on the other hand, does not like unions but is afraid that if he does not allow an election, the union may set up picket lines and even organize a boycott. He doesn't want any trouble and is afraid of bad publicity. And so he also agrees to have an election and abide by the decision.

Both men agree to hold elections. Yet their attitude and motivation for the decision were different. Whose motivation seemed to be higher? Which one do you feel had a more developed sense of Christian morality? Can you see a difference between being person-centered and law-centered?

Each of us has personal moral decisions to make each day. Too often we ask the wrong questions. Should I lie or not? Should I reveal that scandalous story about my co-worker? How far can I go and still not sin? We need to penetrate much deeper than the surface.

4. CONSCIENCE FORMATION

After graduation from high school, Linda, a young woman from a small town in Kansas, decided to move to New York City, where she got a job and began living on her own. After working for three years with a large insurance company, she met Steve, an employee of the same company. After a relatively brief perod of time, they became engaged and were married.

A mutual friend had first introduced Linda and Steve. Many of Linda's co-workers talked about Steve. Invariably their description of Steve would include the word *conscientious*. Linda often reflected on what others had to say about him. Loving him as she did, she liked it very much when others would say that Steve was conscientious.

After their marriage Linda found herself describing Steve to her friends as one of the most conscientious persons she had ever known. When asked to explain what she meant, Linda would say things such as:

> Steve is an excellent provider; he is as honest as the day is long. He is a responsible person and very sensitive to myself and the needs of others. He is trusted and respected at work, in the community, and at church. His faithfulness to me and our family is unquestionable. Steve never jumps to conclusions; he thinks things through, and when he is satisfied that he has arrived at the answer, he acts on his decision. I find great comfort and strength in his maturity.
>
> Steve has a great concern for the people of the world. The life of any human is important to him. He is concerned with hunger, poverty, and war and has been known to speak out freely, even when it is not the popular thing to do. I guess I would say he is loved very much by many because he himself loves so much.

Calling Steve a conscientious person has seemed to say so many things. It implies maturity and responsibility. When one hears Linda talk about Steve, one is hearing about a person who has formed his conscience and who acts upon it. He really uses the conscience in the best sense. It is obvious that such a fully formed conscience did not just happen to Steve. Nor was it something that Steve created overnight. It was a gradual process of a lifetime. Steve benefited from the help of others but worked a lot of this out himself. Keeping in mind the story of Linda and Steve, let us explore the process of conscience formation.

The formation of a person's conscience does not happen to an individual overnight. It is an ongoing process throughout life that occurs during a person's lived experiences. Many factors are involved which enter into the process. The formation of conscience involves three stages: awareness, discernment, and decision.

The stage of awareness finds a person developing a sense of values. People begin to realize that they are responsible for their actions. Some actions ought to be done; others ought to be avoided. When a person is judged innocent by reason of insanity, the law is recognizing that this individual is incapable of distinguishing right from wrong. No values were developed. This sense of values begins when one is a child. The disciplining by parents enables that child to begin developing this sense. Gradually people acquire a sense of responsibility for their actions and an ability to make clear decisions for which they are willing to be accountable.

As people mature with this awareness that values need to be developed, they begin the process of discernment. What precisely are the things I should or should not do? It is a quest for the truth, the correct way of acting. This quest is never-ending. As Christians our basis of morality is the law of Christ. The moral law of loving God and neighbor should be our guide. In applying the law of Christ concretely to our everyday actions, we seek the enlightenment of others. It may be our confessor. It may be people whom we respect. It may be in books we read. The teachings of the Church and specifically those of the Pope should be consulted. While none of these are infallible guides, they do help us come to decisions that are carefully thought out. What is important is that whatever conciusions we reach, they are reached because we see in them the truth. Our opinions may not be infallible, but they are all we have to live on. It is indeed the truth as we perceive it.

Finally comes the stage of decision. This is conscience acting in its real sense. When we are confronted with a situation in the here-and-now, the conscience is our only guide. In the second stage we were simply setting up our moral norms. Stealing is wrong. Giving money to the poor is right. We should not be lying. But now it is the conscience telling me what I must do or not do right now. It does not matter what anybody else has said in the past about certain actions. The question is: What is my conscience telling me right now? When it involves a particular decision in this way, the conscience is infallible. To fail to follow what my conscience tells me right now would be wrong—even if everyone else in the world feels otherwise. In the *Constitution on the Church in the Modern World* Vatican II says:

> Conscience is the most secret core and sanctuary of man. There he is alone with God, whose voice echoes in his depths. In a wonderful manner conscience reveals that law which is fulfilled by love of God and neighbor. In fidelity to conscience, Christians are joined with the rest of men in the search for truth and for the genuine solution to the numerous problems which arise in the life of individuals and from social relationships. Conscience frequently errs from invincible ignorance

without losing its dignity. The same cannot be said of a man who cares but little for truth and goodness, or of a conscience which by degrees grows practically sightless as a result of habitual sin (n. 14).

Catechists often deal with conscience formation during sacramental preparation programs. It is often found that in talking with the parents much has been left to the Church. People tend to seek the answers to these moral questions from "Father." If "Father" says it, it must be so. Little thought is given to the individual's freedom in acting on one's own. What is misunderstood is that when an individual is impelled by another, there is no freedom. Thomas Aquinas once said:

> He who avoids evil not because it is evil, but because a precept of the Lord forbids it, is not free. On the other hand, he who avoids evil because it is evil is free.

Conscience is basically defined as the ability to see the difference between right and wrong. This ability is attributed functionally to the intellect, and the emphasis is often on the rational, cognitive, or "knowing" factors: conscience, knowing what is right or wrong, e.g. a "nagging" conscience, is the intellect or judging power telling you that something you are doing is wrong. Conscience deals with what one has to do.

Christian conscience encompasses all that has been written and includes much more. In Christian conscience the stress is on action or Christian witness. It is the habitual force within me that awakens me to the needs of my brothers and sisters and motivates me to do something about them. Christian conscience is found within the Christian community and is sensitive to that community. Recognizing that Christian living is God-centered and community-centered, Christian conscience acts in humility. Being love-oriented, Christian conscience goes beyond the world of the law (the required) to the world of aspiration (the possible). The real motivation of Christian actions is thus not avoidance.

Christian conscience is therefore that which directs and orients our relations with other persons; it alerts us to the actions and reactions of others. It is thus developed by practice, not just by increasing one's knowledge. In *A Curriculum Guide for Continuous Progress in Religious Education,* the NCEA National Conference of Directors of Religious Education describes well the fully integrated Christian who has formed his or her conscience in light of the law of Christ:

> The end product of Christian education is the person:
> Who is aware of his own worth
> including an understanding of his identity
> and integrity as a human person, with thoughts, feelings,
> desires, and actions . . .
> > and including an understanding of his
> > relationship with the Father, through the Son
> > and in the Spirit.

Who is conscious of the social dimensions of
his life through a deepening of his relationships
to his family, friends, the larger communities . . .
    and through a special deepening of his
    relationship to God in the social context of the Church
    and with a vision of the wider kingdom of God.

Who is open to all of human experience,
taking part in the communication process
which reveals and promotes truth, beauty,
goodness, and responding with a healthy
sense of celebration . . .
and open to the gift of faith
taking part in the communication process wherein
God reveals himself in Jesus, Church, creation,
and responding with love and worship.

Who is growing in his consciousness of values
and in his ability to choose, to prize, to act,
according to that which is good . . .
    and who is growing in his consciousness of
    the redemptive meaning of Christian values,
    especially the invitations of the Gospel,
    and in his ability
    to live by these values,
    to respond to human need with faith and concern,
    to share in the transformation of the world.

Who is maturing as a responsible person
who freely exercises choices on life's options
the choices he has made . . .
    and who is maturing as a Christian person
    who is continually open to God's will and
    responsibility for his choices—
    a person whose faith life really makes a difference.

QUESTIONS FOR REFLECTION

1. Try to reflect on some very difficult moral choice which you have had to make. Can you pick out the stages of awareness, discernment, and decision?

2. What were the competing values which made it such a difficult decison?

3. Why is conscience formation more than simply doing what Father says is right?

4. How do you see the relationship between conscience and the authority of the Church?

Unit Seven

WE ENCOUNTER GOD THROUGH OTHERS

1. THE PROPHETS AND THEIR SOCIAL MESSAGE

What do you think of when you hear the word "prophet"? It has different meanings for different persons—a fortune teller, a visionary, a forecaster of the future, a holy man. All of these different connotations arise from a common source: the prophets of Israel. To understand the whole idea of prophets and prophecy, it is important to look at the culture of Israel.

Communication outside of shouting range existed long before the coming of post offices, telephone companies, and telegraph offices. In fact, communication even took place before there was any written literature. If a king wished to send a message to another king in pre-literary times, he would send the message through a courier. This person would memorize exactly what the king said. When he arrived at the palace of the other king, the messenger would say to him: "Thus says my lord, the king: 'I the king say to you. . . .'" Then he would repeat the message in the first person as if the king himself were really present.

Ancient peoples saw their gods very much as they did their kings. Like the kings these gods also sent messengers to communicate orally to the people their messages. Just as there was often a king more important than the others, so these peoples saw one god as more important than the others. That god would gather together his council to discuss different matters and make decisions. After the meeting he would send messengers to deliver orally his messages to other lesser gods as the king does.

To describe God's dealing with Israel, the sacred writers adapted the Canaanite mythology to their situation. Since Israel held to a strict monotheism, there could no longer be a reference to a most important god and lesser gods; there was one God alone: Yahweh. When he met in council with his advisors, instead of lesser gods, they were called "angels," or messengers. Just as it was not fitting for the king himself to deliver his own messages, neither was it for Yahweh. God sent his angels to deliver his messages to his human subjects. Prophets came to Israel when, instead of angels, God sent human beings to deliver God's message to Israel.

A prophet then could be called the messenger, or mouthpiece, of Yahweh. The one thing that unites all prophets is that they were spokespersons for God. In this chapter our attention will be centered on the latter prophets, those who wrote down their works. The era of the prophets coincides almost exactly with the era of the kings of Israel. The function of the prophets seemed to be that of calling the people to fidelity to the covenant. Their fidelity was usually dependent on the fidelity of the king. Therefore, in order to appreciate what any of the prophets had to say, it is important to find out when the prophet wrote, where the prophet wrote, and what kind of person the king was.

The prophecies seemed to have a common literary form. They begin with the commissioning of the messenger. The prophet must establish his credentials to convince the people that he is speaking for God. The prophet is basically saying that he has stood before the council of Yahweh. In Isaiah 6 the prophet describes the council where he stood when he received his commission. Ezekiel 1–3 uses similar vivid imagery. Jeremiah 1 speaks of a dialogue between Yahweh and the prophet. Although he does not use imagery or dialogue, Amos refers to his call by Yahweh, and, similar to the other prophets, Jeremiah denounces the false prophets because they were *not* present at the council of Yahweh:

> I did not send these prophets,
>   yet they ran;
> I did not speak to them,
>   yet they prophesied.
> Had they stood in my council,
>   and did they but proclaim to my people my words,
> They would have brought them back from evil ways
>   and from their wicked deeds (Jer 23:21–22).

Since the prophets' message to the people concerns their infidelity to the covenant, the prophet very often sounds like a prosecuting attorney. The courtroom is in heaven and Yahweh is the judge. The council is the jury. The law is the decalogue. The judge and jury find the people guilty, and the prophet must bring the decision of Yahweh to the people. So the prophet brings forth the accusations with the evidence and announces the judgment. This literary form is called a *rib* or lawsuit. It takes up all of 1 and 2 Kings. Almost all of the kings are found guilty of infidelity to the covenant.

The covenant is such a central theme in all the prophets that it can be related to virtually any of their messages. When a prophet such as Isaiah speaks of a future messiah of the line of David, it is in reference to the covenant Yahweh made. When Jeremiah foretells doom and destruction to the nation, it is because the people have not been faithful to the covenant.

If this relationship to covenant theology is kept in mind, it is natural that many of the prophets would call the people to task for their failure in social justice. Although God led all of Israel as a group from slavery to freedom, Israel had failed and was no longer providing equal justice for all. Because God dealt with Israel as a people, the people are expected to have a sensitivity to the whole community. Above all, failure in social justice is a sign that the people really have neglected God. Oppressing and maltreating others out of a desire to enrich themselves occurs precisely because Israel has lost sight of God who had liberated them and to whom they should turn for help. Independence and individualism lead to oppression of others.

As we look at a few of the prophets who face the issues of social justice, keep in mind existing parallels today. Rugged individualism, self-seeking, and autonomy are no less present in our society than in that of Israel.

Amos. The earliest of the "latter" or "classical" prophets was a man named Amos. A shepherd from Tekoa in the southern kingdom of Judah, he was called by God to prophesy against the northern kingdom of Israel. This took place during the reign of Jeroboam II (786–746 B.C.). It was a time of national prosperity, yet there was indifference to the plight of the poor.

Amos directed his attention to the social evils of the day, particularly the dishonesty and heartlessness with which the rich had trampled on the poor (2:6f; 5:10–12; 8:4–6). He also pointed out the immorality and careless pursuit of luxury which was making the nation soft (2:7f; 4:1–3; 6:1–6). There had developed a certain complacency. Israel felt that since she was a chosen people, she was guaranteed God's protection (1; 2; 3:1f; 9:7), and the obligations of the covenant were fulfilled by mere external worship (5:21–29). Amos declared that Israel's cult had become a place of sin at which Yahweh was not present (4:4f; 5:1–6). The only future Amos saw in Israel was utter ruin.

Hosea. Hosea was practically a contemporary of Amos, except that he lived in the northern kingdom of Israel. He came to his prophetic call through a tragic experience. His wife Gomer, whom he loved very much, abandoned him for a life of prostitution, possibly taking part in the fertility rites of the pagan cult. Reflecting on his own situation, Hosea prophesied on the covenant between Israel and Yahweh as being like a marriage bond. Israel in worshiping other gods was guilty of "adultery" and therefore faced "divorce," national ruin (2:2–13). Hosea denounced the Baal worship and all the moral corruption that paganism entailed (4:1–14; 6:8–10; 8:5f). Because Israel had forgotten all the saving deeds of Yahweh (11:1–4; 13:4–8), she was no longer his people. Because Hosea did not see in Israel any sign of true repentance for her crimes (5:15—6:6; 7:14–16), Hosea, like Amos, saw doom for the nation (7:13; 9:11–17).

Hosea's patience and enduring love for his wife finally paid off. His wife repented and returned to him. Just as Hosea forgave and rehabilitated Gomer (ch. 3), Yahweh in his faithful love would one day forgive Israel and restore the covenant bond (2:14–23; 11:8–11; 14:1–8). But this was to occur only after the destruction of Israel.

Isaiah. Called to the prophetic ministry (6:1) in the year of King Uzziah's death (742 B.C.), Isaiah for fifty years exerted his influence during the reigns of Kings Jotham, Ahaz, and Hezekiah. Most of Isaiah's preaching took place in Jerusalem. Overwhelmed through his inaugural experience (ch. 6) both by the profound holiness of Yahweh and the depth of national sin, Isaiah first delivered a message of denunciation. He attacked the powerful and heartless nobles and the corrupt judges who colluded to deprive the helpless of their rights (1:21–23; 3:13–15; 5:8; 23; 10:1–4). He was especially harsh toward the decadent wealthy, who were only interested in acquiring wealth and pursuing pleasure (3:16—4:1; 5:11f; 22). They had neither principles of morality nor faith in God (5:18–21). Like his contemporaries to the north, Amos and Hosea, Isaiah felt that the people were beyond correction (6:9f) and declared that the empty rituals of Judah were not acceptable to Yahweh (1:10–20). The day of Yahweh was to come as a day of judgment (2:6–21), and the Assyrian army would be that instrument (5:26–29). Isaiah saw the nation crumbling internally (3:1–12), falling into ruin, and reduced to a tiny remnant (10:22f)—and even that remnant would be laid waste (6:13).

Because Isaiah's prophecy about the virgin birth is probably the one most well known to people, it is appropriate to comment on it. Isaiah like the other prophets was preaching fidelity to the covenant. The people should trust in Yahweh alone. The kingdom of Judah was under attack by Syria and Israel because Ahaz refused to enter into an alliance with these two kingdoms against Assyria. But Ahaz, fearful of the attack, is not willing to trust in Yahweh's protective power and decides to enter into alliance with Assyria. Isaiah tells Ahaz to ask for a sign from Yahweh to show that Judah will be protected. Ahaz refuses. In response Isaiah says:

> Listen, O house of David! Is it not enough for you to weary men, must you also weary my God? Therefore the Lord himself will give you this sign: the virgin shall be with child, and bear a son, and shall name him Immanuel. He shall be living on curds and honey by the time he learns to reject the bad and choose the good. For before the child learns to reject the bad and choose the good, the land of those two kings whom you dread will be deserted (7:13–16).

Matthew's Gospel takes this prophecy as a reference to the birth of Jesus from the Virgin Mary. In the original text the Hebrew word means "young woman" or "maiden." While not denying the virgin birth, we should realize that Isaiah did not have Jesus in mind. More likely it is a prophecy of the birth of Hezekiah as well as a reminder that fidelity to the covenant means not allying with foreign kingdoms. It is Matthew's thought and Christian reflection that give this prophecy its full meaning.

Whenever we refer to the writings of the prophet of Isaiah, only chapters 1–39 of the book of Isaiah are included. The succeeding chapters were written by different persons at a much later date. In their written form all the different writings were put under the one heading of "Isaiah," perhaps because the subsequent compilers and editors were of an Isaian school.

Micah. Like Isaiah, Micah prophesied in the late eighth century in the southern kingdom, especially Jerusalem. With fiery zeal he attacked the rich who exploited the poor, the fradulent merchants, and the compromising judges, as well as the corrupt priests and prophets. Micah himself came from the country, a tiny village of Meresheth in the foothills. Thus he saw the vices of the nation to be centered in the city of Jerusalem. King Ahaz had allowed pagan practices to take place. The worship of Yahweh declined.

Micah felt that since paganism necessarily involved a breach of Yahweh's covenant, it eventually led to a disregard of covenant law, which was the foundation of society and guarantee of human rights. Micah pointed out the consequent social ills. The great landowners dishonestly and coldly evict the poor (2:1–2, 9). Because the rulers are corrupt, the poor have no one to appeal to (3:1–4, 9–10). At the same time the wealthy live in luxury without any concern for the abysmal condition of their less fortunate brothers and sisters. The clergy and the prophets see their work as only a way to earn a living (3:11). Micah states very concisely his mission:

> But as for me, I am filled with power,
>   with the spirit of the Lord,
>   with authority and with might,
> To declare to Jacob his crimes
>   and to Israel his sins (3:8).

Jeremiah. Jeremiah was born around 650 of a priestly family near Jerusalem in a little village named Anathoth. His call as a prophet occurred in the thirteenth year of King Josiah (628) of the kingdom of Judah. Josiah was a reformer, but the reforms never were fully realized due to Josiah's death in 609. The era of good feeling was over for Jeremiah. Idolatry returned to Judah. The people knew God's law but did not heed his word (8:8f). The clergy made peace offerings for a people guilty of atrocious crimes against the covenant (6:13–15; 8:10–12; 7:5–11). The ritual was empty (7:21–23) and the reforms insincere (4:3f; 8:4–7).

Because Jeremiah spoke out so boldly and forcefully, he suffered. He was accused of blasphemy and treason, for he had condemned King Jehoiakim for his pursuit of luxury (22:13–15). The king wanted a better palace than the other kings. Jeremiah almost broke under the pressure (15:15–18; 18:19–23), but he said that he just could not remain silent (20:9). Somehow he always found strength to go on (15:19–20).

Jeremiah exercised his prophetic ministry for an extremely long period of time. His early career took place during a high point of Jewish history, the reign of Josiah. It was at that time that there were undertaken the reforms of the Jewish law and a rededication to the covenant. But his later career saw the gradual moral decay and corruption leading eventually to the demise of Judah and the deportation of the Jews to Babylon. With perseverance and courage against determined opposition Jeremiah prophesied boldly till his death. His own words tell us very beautifully his difficulties as well as his strength:

> You duped me, O Lord, and I let myself be duped;
>   you were too strong for me, and you triumphed.
> All the day I am an object of laughter;
>   everyone mocks me.
>
> Whenever I speak, I must cry out,
>   violence and outrage is my message;
> The word of the Lord has brought me
>   derision and reproach all the day.
>
> I say to myself, I will not mention him,
>   I will speak in his name no more.
> But then it becomes like fire burning in my heart,
>   imprisoned in my bones.
> I grow weary holding it in,
>   I cannot endure it.
>
> Yes, I hear the whisperings of many:
>   "Terror on every side!
>   Denounce! Let us denounce him!"
> All those who were my friends
>   are on the watch for any misstep of mine.
> "Perhaps he will be trapped; then we can prevail,
>   and take our vengeance on him."
>
> But the Lord is with me, like a mighty champion:
>   my persecutors will stumble, they will not triumph.
> In their failure they will be put to utter shame,
>   to lasting, unforgettable confusion (20:7–11).

The classical prophets all had their own background, culture, personality, and way of life, and their message differed in many ways. Yet there were some common themes: denunciation of the sins of society, the worship of false gods, and the empty ritual. They were all related to the need of fidelity to the covenant. The prophets called to mind Yahweh's saving deeds toward his people and the covenant which he established to signify that relationship. The prophets then saw the need to obey scrupulously all the stipulations attached to the covenant. The people were to worship Yahweh alone and obey his covenant law in all dealings with their Israelite neighbors. The way the prophets evaluated Israelite society was seen in this light. The judgment to come which the prophets pronounced was a consequence of that evaluation. As in the days of the prophets, social justice today is an integral part of the message of salvation, for to live a loving relationship with God is to strive to attain in one's society a community of equity and justice for all.

QUESTIONS FOR REFLECTION

1. What are the common personality traits of these three prophets? What persons of our age reflect these same traits? How?

2. Which personality traits do you feel you possess? Which do you lack?

3. The prophets were constantly calling the people to be faithful to the covenant. In view of Jesus' universal call to salvation, what would covenant fidelity mean to us today?

2. COMMUNAL NATURE OF SIN

In many of the chapters of this book we have come across the term "covenant." The Bible itself is divided into two sections, the Old Testament and the New Testament, the word testament meaning covenant. Covenant is the clearest expression to us of God's relationship with us. The very identity of Israel as a people was based on the covenant which God made. Jesus' death and resurrection brought about a new covenant. We became "a chosen race, a royal priesthood, a holy nation, a people (God) claims for his own" (1 Pt 2:9). Our salvation by Jesus Christ came to us as a solidarity, a community of the saved.

Grace and salvation are seen in this communal dimension. Sin also must be seen in this communal dimension. As there is a solidarity of grace, there also is a solidarity of sin. When we as individuals sin, its effects redound on the community. St. Paul uses the analogy of the body to describe our oneness in salvation.

The weaknesses as well as the strengths of one part of the body affect the entire body.

> If one member suffers, all the members suffer with it; if one member is honored, all the members share its joy (1 Cor 12:26).

It is so easy to think of sin only in an individualistic way. "It is *my* sin. *I* offended God. *I* broke his law." This narrow outlook toward sin often stems from looking at sin from an excessively legalistic viewpoint. Such a view would define sin as *a free and deliberate transgression of God's law.* "I lied. I missed Mass. I disobeyed my parents. I cheated." My outlook then becomes only a concern with how I offended God.

A more appropriate view of sin should consider the two great commandments of love and how Jesus showed us the relationship between the two. With such a view sin might be described as *the deliberate violation of God's law to love.* We are willfully refusing to share God's love with others. We are refusing to be open with others. As in the above paragraph, I may be doing something against God's law. But my attention is not centered on the law as such. It is on the relationships I have damaged, the persons I have affected.

Let's take a look at the same action and compare the contrasting views of sin. I cheat on my income tax. With the individualistic view of sin, I have disobeyed the fourth commandment because I am not respecting civil authorities. Or perhaps what I did was against the commandment not to steal. However, with a communal view of sin, I realize that what I have done has been to hurt those around me. They in effect are paying taxes for me. I am weakening my share in supporting the community. I am not working with my sisters and brothers in a common endeavor. What I have done affects others.

A common failing is gossip. From an individualist view of sin, the sin may involve destroying the good name of another. From a communal view, it involves the undermining of a positive attitude which we should have for one another. If we do not work to strengthen and support one another, we are not building an effective community. People begin to distrust one another. Such a negative attitude spreads like cancer.

Just as every sin is basically communal, there are many actions communal in origin which are much more destructive than an individual's action against another individual. In racial segregation, for example, because people of different races live apart from one another, intolerance and bigotry develop. One race may be privileged, the other deprived. One ends up significantly wealthier and better educated than the other. Who is responsible? No one person. But it is an evil in the society. And as such it is a sin for which society is responsible. Maybe every individual in the privileged race can say: "I don't hate these people. I have always treated them well. I would never do anything to hurt them." Yet the evil persists. When no one is able to claim responsibility, the responsibility lies with everyone.

Jesus was often accused of associating with sinners. He asked the tax-collector Matthew to be his disciple. He forgave the swindling Zacchaeus. He intervened to save the woman caught in adultery. He befriended Mary Magdalene.

He said he came to save not the self-righteous but sinners. Yet where he seemed to be most intolerant was in the area of social sins. The people who seemed so self-righteous when an individual sin was committed were often the very ones who were destructive of the social order. Jesus did not criticize the *actions* of these people. He criticized their *attitude*. They failed to have a sense of sin in the social sense.

In no place does Jesus express more strongly the importance of love of neighbor than in his discourse on the last judgment. He goes so far as to condemn to eternal punishment those who neglect their brothers or sisters in need:

> " 'Out of my sight, you condemned, into that everlasting fire prepared for the devil and his angels! I was hungry and you gave me no food, I was thirsty and you gave me no drink. I was away from home and you gave me no welcome, naked and you gave me no clothing. I was ill and in prison and you did not come to comfort me.' Then they in turn will ask: 'Lord, when did we see you hungry or thirsty or away from home or naked or ill or in prison and not attend you in your needs?' He will answer them: 'I assure you, as often as you neglected to do it to one of these least ones, you neglected to do it to me.' These will go off to eternal punishment and the just to eternal life" (Mt 25:41–46).

Jesus came to redeem a people. Therefore, his concern was to overturn the conditions in society which reflected a sinful, unredeemed people. He was involved with so much controversy with the Jewish leaders because they represented the obstacle for changing the society. When the attitude of a people is changed, the individuals themselves are more readily inclined to change.

As a culture within our own society, we need to address sin in its communal dimension. If, for example, all we see in poverty is individuals deprived of goods or out of work, we may only direct our attention to giving individuals food stamps or another job. But if we begin to see poverty as an evil for which we all have a responsibility, our concerted effort begins to be directed at some of the root causes within our society.

The more we think of community in our actions, the more we are cooperating in the plan of redemption. As a group of worshiping Christians, we need to examine our faults not just in light of what *I* did wrong but also in terms of its effects on others: how it affected the family within which I make my home, how it affected the people with whom I work, how it affected the parish community within which I worship, and how it affected the society within which I live. As we are able to do that, we become less self-centered and more Christ-centered. We will be able to be counted among those on the right to whom the king says:

> " 'Come, you have my Father's blessing! Inherit the kingdom prepared for you from the creation of the world. For I was hungry and you gave me food. I was thirsty and you gave me drink. I was a stranger and you

welcomed me, naked and you clothed me. I was ill and you comforted me, in prison and you came to visit me. . . . As often as you did it for one of my least brothers, you did it for me' " (Mt 25:34–40).

QUESTIONS FOR REFLECTION

1. Examine yourself. How does an awareness of the communal dimension of your sins enable you to be more effectively healed?
___
___
___
___

2. How are you able to deal with the sins of society which you encounter?
___
___
___
___

3. Examine some specific evil which you see in your neighborhood or community. How do you and your community respond to make it better? Give some specific ways.
___
___
___
___

4. In what ways have you experienced hurt through others either individually or communally? How might this hurt be healed? Who would do it?
___
___
___
___

3. CATHOLIC TEACHING ON SOCIAL JUSTICE

The United States of America is a country endowed with wealth unsurpassed in the world. Its gross national product exceeding one trillion dollars is twice the amount of the Soviet Union. Over ninety percent of all families in our country own television sets. Even the poor own automobiles. What is termed poverty in the United States would be considered affluence in other countries.

Two-thirds of the world's people are living in extreme poverty or dying from hunger. For a person who has never known extreme hunger and never even seen such suffering, it is difficult to have compassion on the multitudes that live their daily lives in constant hunger. When one has lived in a relatively free country such as ours, it is difficult to imagine the feeling of living under oppression. Although our very affluence may be the cause of oppression and exploitation in another country, we are able successfully to insulate ourselves as if the problem did not exist.

Even in the United States segments of society have been ignored. Laws, designed in theory to preserve the "inalienable rights" of its people, have been written that have become means of oppression, violation of the rights of some of its citizens, and segregation. When enough concern over such unjust situations has occurred, laws have been repealed or new laws enacted that have alleviated inequities or oppressive situations. The process of reform is possible. The United States may not have attained the perfect society, but it is a country that affords more freedom than any other country in the world. Such freedom compels us to become aware of the injustice that exists around us each day. We as a free people are accountable for these injustices.

It is when we are faced not only with the injustices, but with the moral obligation to do something about them as Christians that we become uncomfortable. To face issues of social justice makes us American Catholics very uncomfortable. We have often turned a deaf ear or squirmed when the Holy Father has spoken on social justice. Pope Paul VI intended to open up such ears in his 1967 encyclical on social justice, *Populorum Progressio,* when he said:

> Would that all who declare themselves Christ's disciples heeded his appeal: "I was hungry and you gave me to eat; I was thirsty and you gave me to drink; I was a stranger and you took me in; naked and you covered me; sick and you visited me; I was in prison and you came to me." No one may look with indifference on the lot of his brothers who are still weighted down by such poverty and afflicted with ignorance and pining away with insecurity. The soul of every Christian must be moved by these miseries as Christ was when he said: "I have compassion on the multitude" (n. 74).

Mother Teresa of Calcutta, Superior General of the Missionaries of Charity, was asked to open a house for her sisters in the Harlem section of Manhattan and work with the poor of the city. After visiting her sisters there, Mother Teresa reported that the difficulty that the sisters had in the United States was determining just who were the poorest of the poor. They did not find hunger, sickness, or the extreme conditions of poverty in Harlem that they found in other parts of the world.

What they did find was the extreme loneliness of the people. Many people were confined to one-room apartments because they were either afraid or too sick to go out even to do their shopping. They were without friends to share their joys and sorrows. They were cared for by no one, abandoned by the rest of society, and left to live and die in extreme loneliness. The prison of loneliness may be different than that of a penal institution, but injustices are certainly present in that situation. Each of us must be aware that we need not look very far to find this very type of situation in our own neighborhoods.

This form of ministry is not confined to Mother Teresa's sisters alone. In Los Angeles the Missionary Brothers of Charity daily minister to the poorest of the poor on skid row: the hungry, the homeless, the imprisoned, the sick. In most major cities of the United States we find a variety of people working individually or for organizations in order to try to bring justice to the poor. There are found halfway houses, homes for abused mothers and children, free medical clinics, hospitality kitchens, senior citizens' centers, day care centers for children, and homes for runaway youth.

On June 1, 1941, the fiftieth anniversary of Pope Leo XIII's famous social encyclical *Rerum Novarum,* Pope Pius XII delivered a Pentecost Sunday message broadcast to the entire Catholic world. His theme was social justice. Besides affirming the perennial validity and inexhaustible worth of the teachings in *Rerum Novarum,* he set down the moral principles underlying three fundamental values of social and economic life: the use of material goods, work, and the family.

Regarding material goods, Pius XII declared that the right of all people to use them for their own sustenance is prior to every other economic right, even that of private property. The right to the private possession of material goods is a natural one; nevertheless, in the objective order established by God, the right to property cannot stand in the way of the more basic principle that "the goods which were created by God for all men should flow to all alike, according to the principles of justice and charity."

Regarding work, our Holy Father repeated the teaching of *Rerum Novarum* that a person's work is both a duty and a right. It is for individuals, therefore, to regulate their relations where their work is concerned. If they cannot do so or will not do so, then, and only then, does "it fall back on the state to intervene in the division and distribution of work, and this must be according to the form and measure that the common property demands."

Regarding the family, the Pope affirmed that the private ownership of material goods has a great part to play in promoting the welfare of family life. It "secures for the father of a family the healthy liberty he needs in order to fulfill the duties assigned him by the Creator regarding the physical, spiritual and religious welfare of the family." It is in this that the right of the families to migrate is rooted. And so, regarding migration, Pius reminded both the countries from which persons are emigrating and those receiving the newcomers that they should seek always "to eliminate as far as possible all obstacles to the birth and growth of real confidence" between the nations. In this way both will contribute to, and share in, the increased welfare of mankind and the progress of culture.

It may seem strange to refer to a message that was delivered in 1941, but we wish to show how little such messages of social concern are heeded. For very soon after Pope Pius XII's radio message, the United States was guilty of violating those very fundamental values of society which the Pope had been upholding. It is the story of Manzanar.

Manzanar was the name of one of the concentration camps in which 10,000 Americans were imprisoned simply because they were of Japanese ancestry. Two-thirds of the 110,000 interred in various concentration camps like Manzanar were American citizens by birth. The rest were first-generation Americans born in Japan but forbidden by law from becoming American citizens. In relocating to this desert camp of Manzanar, they were forced to abandon their homes, property, and businesses. All of this came about by executive order 9066, signed by President Franklin Roosevelt on February 19, 1942. It was barely two months after Pearl Harbor, and anti-Japanese hysteria was running wild.

Evacuees were usually given seven to ten days to complete their business before being sent first to an assembly center, then to an internment camp. They were only allowed to take with them what they were able to carry in the evacuation. Although many stored the rest of their possessions in local Japanese temples and churches or in garages and sheds belonging to neighbors, this action was virtually useless. A postwar survey indicated that eighty percent of these privately stored goods were rifled, stolen or sold during their internment.

The touch of irony to this injustice is that thousands of young Japanese volunteered for active duty in the armed forces, and many joined the war industries to serve their country. One of the most heroic fighting units of the war was the 442nd regimental combat team, composed of Americans of Japanese ancestry. The inhabitants of these concentration camps even included those Japanese Americans who had served honorably in World War I.

On June 30, 1946, the last relocation center was closed, but it did not end the issue of concentration camps in the United States. The authorization for them was still on the books for another thirty years. On February 19, 1976, President Gerald Ford formally rescinded executive order 9066. It was only then that fear was dispelled that this unfortunate episode in history could occur again.

The memory of Manzanar is still very much alive in the minds and hearts of many Japanese Americans who were interned there and in other camps. In 1973 Manzanar was designated a California historical landmark. Inscribed on the plaque are the words: "May the injustices and humiliation suffered here as a result of hysteria, racism, and economic exploitation never emerge again."

On Pentecost Sunday Pius XII had spoken on the three fundamental values of social and economic life: material goods, work, and the family. Only eight months later the United States violated those very rights by the establishment of a series of "Manazars" for the internment of over 110,000 people. They were deprived of their right to material goods, their ability to work, and their ability to promote the welfare of family life. This is only one of many instances of humanity's injustice to one another.

It is such incidents of oppression that the Church has addressed throughout its history. Each of us as Christians must be awakened to the reality of the injustices that exist in our homes, neighborhoods, cities, states, country, and the world. We must stand up and be counted in opposition to any situation that exploits, unjustly discriminates, or permits any form of injustice to exist. We must discontinue "lip service" while reflecting and responding to the call of the prophet Micah:

> You have been told, O man, what is good,
>   and what the Lord requires of you:
> Only to do the right and to love goodness,
>   and to walk humbly with your God (Mi 6:8).

To reflect on these very meaningful words of Scripture, one is immediately called to recognize that *the Lord requires* of each of us to *do the right,* not "lip service" but action on behalf of our sisters and brothers, whoever they might be. The Lord requires not only that we *love* but that it be a love of *goodness,* a love for all people we meet in each and every circumstance of our lives. Finally the Lord asks that we not only *walk* but that we *walk humbly* with our *God.* To respond to the Lord's request clearly calls on each of us to be persons committed to issues of justice, willing to show by our actions and our love for one another that we are capable of not only walking with our God but walking humbly with him.

Throughout its history the Catholic Church has clearly stated its position in the areas of social justice. The Gospel message has been re-presented in the area of social justice especially in this last century as new issues of social concern have arisen. The social encyclicals have included the following:

> *Rerum Novarum*, Pope Leo XIII (1891)
> *Quadragesimo Anno*, Pope Pius XI (1931)
> *Mater et Magistra*, Pope John XXIII (1961)
> *Pacem in Terris*, Pope John XXIII (1963)
> *Ecclesiam Suam*, Pope Paul VI (1964)
> *Populorum Progressio*, Pope Paul VI (1967)

When the bishops of the world met for the Second Vatican Council, there was a schema of decrees and constitutions for them to draw up and approve. The one document that was not on the schema was the *Pastoral Constitution on the Church in the Modern World (Gaudium et Spes).* It was conceived within the deliberations of the Council itself because of the pressing need for the Church to face in a positive way the issues of the modern world in light of the Gospel. Regarding social justice, *Gaudium et Spes* calls each of us to take seriously the problems, to spend time in reflection, and then to follow that course of action consistent with our person. We are always to have compassion on the multitudes and to work to alleviate the misery of peoples in the world, responding to Jesus' command to love one another as we love ourselves:

> Meanwhile there is a growing conviction of mankind's ability and duty to strengthen its mastery over nature and of the need to establish a political, social and economic order at the service of man to assert and develop the dignity proper to individuals and to society.
>
> As a result very many persons are quite aggressively demanding those benefits of which with vivid awareness they judge themselves to be deprived either through injustices or unequal distribution. Nations on the road to progress, like those recently made independent, desire to participate in goods of modern civilization, not only in the political field but also economically, and to play their part freely on the world scene. Still they continually fall behind while very often their dependence on wealthier nations deepens more rapidly, even in the economic sphere.
>
> People hounded by hunger call upon those better off. Where they have not yet won it, women claim for themselves an equity with men before the law and in fact. Laborers and farmers seek not only to provide for the necessities of life but to develop the gifts of their personality by their labors, and indeed to take part in regulating economic, social, political, and cultural life. Now, for the first time in human history, all people are convinced that the benefits of culture ought to be and actually can be extended to everyone.
>
> Still, beneath all these demands lies a deeper and most widespread longing. Persons and societies thirst for a full and free life worthy of man—one in which they can subject to their own welfare all that the modern world can offer them so abundantly. In addition, nations try harder every day to bring about a kind of universal community.
>
> Since all these things are so, the modern world shows itself at once powerful and weak, capable of the noblest deeds or the foulest. Before it lies the path to freedom or to slavery, to progress or retreat, to brotherhood or hatred. Moreover, man is becoming aware that it is his responsibility to guide aright the forces which he has unleashed and which can enslave him or minister to him. That is why he is putting questions to himself (n. 9).

QUESTIONS FOR REFLECTION

Let's take a look at the last paragraph of the statement we have just read: In light of that:

1. What are the questions we should be looking at as persons living in the modern world?

2. How does the modern world show itself as powerful?

3. What are the noble deeds of the modern world?

4. What are the foulest deeds of the modern world?

5. What are the paths of freedom in the modern world?

6. What are the paths of slavery in the modern world?

7. What are the signs of progress in the modern world?

8. What are the signs of retreat in the modern world? _____
_____
_____
_____
_____

9. What are the signs of brotherhood in the modern world? _____
_____
_____
_____
_____

10. What are the signs of hate in the modern world? _____
_____
_____
_____
_____

11. What are the forces unleashed by modern man? _____
_____
_____
_____
_____

12. How are they able to minister to modern man? _____
_____
_____
_____
_____

13. How are they able to enslave modern man? _____
_____
_____
_____
_____

4. SACRAMENTS OF HEALING

The year was 1974. Tommy John, a pitcher for the Los Angeles Dodgers, was having the best season of his career. It was only July, and his record was already 13 wins and 3 losses. He was practically unbeatable. Then in the midst of a game John suddenly walked off the pitcher's mound. No one else knew why at the time, but Tommy John felt something snap in his elbow. His left arm was virtually useless. It seemed that his career as a pitcher had come to an end.

An orthopedic surgeon, Dr. Robert Kerlan, cut into the arm and, through transplanting and other intricate work, restructured the arm. The prognosis was that at best Tommy John might be able to use the arm as long as he didn't lift anything heavy. As far as baseball was concerned, that was completely out of the question. Yet Tommy still felt he could return to baseball. He doggedly underwent a program of therapy and exercised endless hours every day, seven days a week. More than a year after his surgery he got to the point where he could pick up a ball. He began practicing. Hours were spent just gripping the ball. Eventually he even could throw a ball. By spring of 1976 Tommy John was ready to report to Vero Beach to join the Dodgers in training. And he made his comeback. By 1978 John was pitching so effectively that he won 20 games. He became known as the man with the bionic arm.

Much of the credit to the healing of a dead arm belongs to Tommy John himself, but he could not have done it by himself. There was his wife who kept urging him onward in therapy when he was discouraged. There was the owner of the Dodgers, Walter O'Malley, who kept Tommy on salary and always gave him hope that he would return one day to pitch for the Dodgers. There were Dodger fans who sent him letters of best wishes and encouragement. All in their own way contributed to the healing process.

What motivates people to do this is that people are not satisfied with sickness and ill health. When something is broken we feel a need to repair it. When a body is weak, we feel a need to make it strong. That which is not complete needs to be made whole. Although disease may be a reality in the world, it is not considered natural. It is something that needs to be corrected.

What motivates people to do this is that people are not satisfied with sickness and ill health. When something is broken we feel a need to repair it. When a body is weak, we feel a need to make it strong. That which is not complete needs to be made whole. Although disease may be a reality in the world, it is not considered natural. It is something that needs to be corrected.

These natural evils have been seen as part of our fallen nature, an effect of original sin. Jesus sees his healing ministry as an integral part of his mission. Although a person's infirmity is not to be construed as a punishment either for a person's sins or the sins of one's parents (see Jn 9:3), nevertheless the healing of infirmities and the forgiveness of sins go hand in hand in Jesus' ministry. They were signs of the coming of God's reign. The cure of the paralytic illustrates the close relationship between healing and forgiveness of sins:

> Then he re-entered the boat, made the crossing, and came back to his own town. There the people at once brought to him a paralyzed man

lying on a mat. When Jesus saw their faith he said to the paralytic, "Have courage, son; your sins are forgiven." At that some of the scribes said to themselves, "The man blasphemes." Jesus was aware of what they were thinking and said: "Why do you harbor evil thoughts? Which is less trouble to say, 'Your sins are forgiven' or 'Stand up and walk'? To help you realize that the Son of Man has authority on earth to forgive sins"—he then said to the paralyzed man—"Stand up! Roll up your mat, and go home." The man stood up and went toward his home. At the sight, a feeling of awe came over the crowd, and they praised God for giving such authority to men (Mt 9:1-8).

The Church has carried on this twofold ministry through two sacraments: reconciliation (penance) and anointing of the sick. The two are closely related. Both involve a cooperation between the minister and the recipient as was necessary between Dr. Kerlan and Tommy John. Both involve the prayer and support of the wider community of the Church.

QUESTIONS FOR REFLECTION

1. Can you recall a time when you needed healing?

2. How did the support of others aid in the healing process?

RECONCILIATION (PENANCE)

Alice was giving a catechist formation course. One of the students, Dolores, seemed very reluctant to become involved in the activities of the learners. She would mainly just sit back in her chair with arms folded tightly or fists clenched. When she said anything, it was to attack the instructor—often quite viciously. She often would make derogatory statements about the Church. This defiance perdured through almost the entire course.

Alice was concerned about Dolores' attitude but decided that the best thing to do was to live with it rather than to confront her. As the course proceeded,

Dolores began asking Alice questions outside of class. Although most of the questions were hostile, Alice patiently answered them as best she could. As the weeks progressed, Alice sensed that there was something deeper inside that was bothering Dolores. Alice could almost feel a deeper, inner turmoil churning violently inside the woman.

Finally some of that turmoil came bubbling to the surface. Dolores asked Alice what she would think if Dolores said that she had been a great sinner. Alice said that all of us are sinners and that Jesus came to save sinners, not the self-righteous. If she looked down on Dolores because of her sins, she would not be living like Jesus. Dolores said that she was a prostitute at one time. Alice replied with such understanding that Dolores was both shocked and relieved. The hurts of the past began to be unfolded.

About a week later Dolores again returned to Alice. This time she said: "I know that this time if I say this to you, you will never want to be with me again." Her hands were clenched in a tight fist. Alice took her hands, opened up the fist, and said: "I can't think of anything that you could possibly have done that would make me reject you. Try me. Trust me." Dolores blurted out, "I am a lesbian," and ran for the door. She could not leave because the door was locked. Alice came over, opened up the clenched fist, then put her arms around Dolores and embraced her. Alice said, "I love you but in a different way than you have experienced. I love you in the same way that Jesus does." The two women just stayed there together crying.

Through Alice's presence, through her understanding, through her sensitivity, she enabled Dolores to open up and be reconciled. Alice could rightly be called a minister of reconciliation. She enabled a broken life to begin to be healed.

> Jesus said to them: "A man had two sons. The younger of them said to his father, 'Father, give me the share of the estate that is coming to me.' So the father divided up the property. Some days later this younger son collected all his belongings and went off to a distant land, where he squandered his money on dissolute living. After he had spent everything, a great famine broke out in that country and he was in dire need. So he attached himself to one of the propertied class of the place, who sent him to his farm to take care of the pigs. He longed to fill his belly with the husks that were fodder for the pigs, but no one made a move to give him anything. Coming to his senses at last, he said: 'How many hired hands at my father's place have more than enough to eat, while here I am starving! I will break away and return to my father, and say to him, Father, I have sinned against God and against you; I no longer deserve to be called your son. Treat me like one of your hired hands.' With that he set off for his father's house. While he was still a long way off, his father caught sight of him and was deeply moved. He ran out to meet him, threw his arms around his neck, and kissed him. The son said to him, 'Father, I have sinned against God and against you; I no longer deserve to be called your son.' The father said to his servants:

'Quick! bring out the finest robe and put it on him; put a ring on his finger and shoes on his feet. Take the fatted calf and kill it. Let us eat and celebrate because this son of mine was dead and has come back to life. He was lost and is found.' Then the celebration began.

"Meanwhile the elder son was out on the land. As he neared the house on his way home, he heard the sound of music and dancing. He called one of the servants and asked him the reason for the dancing and the music. The servant answered, 'Your brother is home, and your father has killed the fatted calf because he has him back in good health.' The son grew angry at this and would not go in; but his father came out and began to plead with him.

"He said to his father in reply: 'For years now I have slaved for you. I never disobeyed one of your orders, yet you never gave me so much as a kid goat to celebrate with my friends. Then, when this son of yours returns after having gone through your property with loose women, you kill the fatted calf for him.'

" 'My son,' replied the father, 'you are with me always, and everything I have is yours. But we had to celebrate and rejoice! This brother of yours was dead, and has come back to life. He was lost, and is found.' "

This parable expresses most clearly all the dynamics involved in sin and reconciliation. The boy had left his father and wasted all his possessions on selfish endeavors. When he had reached the depths of degradation, he began to examine his past deeds. He acknowledged his sins and really felt sorrow for them. Greatly desiring to receive his father's forgiveness, he repented and returned home to seek his father's forgiveness.

The father on his part wanted nothing more than to see his son again. When he saw the boy from afar, even before the boy had a chance to say anything, the father ran down and greeted him with a warm embrace of reconciliation. Then the boy confessed. The father led a celebration of reconciliation in thanksgiving for the return of his son. In general, the community celebrated with him. Only the older brother had difficulty in forgiving the prodigal son.

All of us have our moments of alienation from one another. Just as sickness calls for healing, alienation calls for reconciliation. Jesus' first words in his public ministry were a call to people to reform their lives:

"This is the time of fulfillment. The reign of God is at hand! Reform your lives and believe in the Gospel" (Mk 1:15).

Jesus called all—even the worst of sinners—to reform. Because of the faith of the person involved, Jesus forgave sins.

When Jesus saw their faith he said to the paralytic, "Have courage, son; your sins are forgiven" (Mt 9:2).

That same kind of faith enabled Jesus to forgive the woman, a known sinner, who had anointed him (Lk 7:50). He gave this power to forgive sins to his disciples:

> Jesus came and stood before them. "Peace be with you," he said. When he had said this, he showed them his hands and his side. At the sight of the Lord the disciples rejoiced. "Peace be with you." he said again.
>
> "As the Father has sent me,
> so I send you."
> Then he breathed on them and said:
> "Receive the Holy Spirit.
> If you forgive men's sins,
> they are forgiven them;
> if you hold them bound,
> they are held bound" (Jn 20:21-23).

Forgiveness goes beyond that internal willingness to conversion after a life of sin. It is to be continuous. As we are able to forgive one another constantly, so will the Father forgive.

> Then Peter came up and asked him, "Lord, when my brother wrongs me, how often must I forgive him? Seven times?" "No," Jesus replied, "not seven times; I say, seven times seven times. . . . My heavenly Father will treat you in exactly the same way unless each of you forgives his brother from his heart" (Mt 18:21-22, 35).

We have said that a sacrament is a living sign by which we encounter a person. The Church has given us a means to encounter the person of Christ as a forgiver and reconciler. The healing, forgiving action of Christ occurs in the sacrament of reconciliation. Although we often refer to it as the sacrament of penance or confession, reconciliation describes more adequately that healing dimension of the sacrament.

In the early years of the Church a separate sacrament for the forgiveness of sins was not a common celebration. It was part of a person's initiation into the Church. Remission of sins was effected through baptism, confirmation, and the Eucharist. But then there eventually came the problem of people who had renounced the way of life into which they had been initiated. What do you do with apostates who are seeking readmission? A rite for the reconciliation of penitents was developed. Those who were public sinners were admitted into the order of penitents because of the scandal they had caused. The three sins which called for this public reconciliation were murder, apostasy, and adultery. Abortion was later included. These were the crimes which were most destructive of community. Murder destroyed the lives of the members. Apostasy undermined the spiritual growth of the community. Adultery undermined the family, the basic unit of the community. The bishop presided at a public ceremony—usually during Lent—at which the community publicly welcomed the penitents back.

The penance was imposed on the sinner before reconciliation. These penances connected with reconciliation were often very severe. Some were known to be imposed for a duration of many years or even a lifetime. It was because of this that many Christians would remain catechumens until their deathbed. Emperor Constantine was an example of this.

The practice of private confession of sins did not begin until the sixth century. The Irish monks introduced the practice. It was to be a number of centuries before it became common practice. Penances became much more lenient (though much stricter than today) and were to be performed after absolution had been granted by the priest.

The practice of confessing in a confessional unseen by the priest is relatively recent. St. Charles Borromeo, Archbishop of Milan, introduced this practice in the sixteenth century. There was to be a grill through which the penitent was still visible. The grill was to be a barrier to prevent any scandal or scandalous accusations involving the confessor and a female penitent. Out of that grill eventually came the obscure screen and confessional box.

Due to these historical developments, the sacrament of reconciliation evolved from a public celebration of the community welcoming back the penitents to the community into a private ordeal in which a sinner confessed his sins to a priest, who, in turn, representing Christ, judging the sinner repentant, granted absolution. Vatican II has called for a reform of this sacrament to reflect its communal dimension. Let's look at the reform in light of the four basic principles for the reform of liturgy.

1. *Liturgy is an action of the whole body of the Church; it is not a private function.* Penance has traditionally been considered the most private of sacraments: a personal thing between the penitent and the priest. Speaking through a screen, penitents confessed their sins, and the priest heard the confession, gave appropriate counsel and a penance (usually a few Our Fathers and Hail Marys), and granted absolution from the sins in the name of Christ. To preserve the confidence, the priest was (and still is) bound to absolute secrecy under the pain of excommunication.

It has been difficult to perceive the action of the Church in this sacrament, so in reforming the sacrament of penance the Church has given us two other rites of reconciliation besides the traditional rite for the reconciliation of individual penitents. These two rites involve communal celebrations of the sacrament. This means that as a group people come together to acknowledge their guilt, examine their consciences, and receive the absolution of the Church. The only difference between the two rites is that in one, within the celebration itself, the penitents confess their sins individually to the priest and receive the priest's absolution. In the other there is only a general confession of sins and general absolution of the priest to the whole community.

Since this last rite represents the most significant change, it is appropriate to comment. Until this rite came out, the Church said that confession of each and every serious sin since the last confession was essential in order to receive the sacrament of penance. The Church now is saying with this rite of general absolution that this is no longer the case. However, some requirements have been laid down regarding general absolution. It may only be granted with the permission of the bishop for a good reason. That usually means too many penitents at the ceremony and not enough priests. Those guilty of serious sin must confess it as soon as reasonably possible and certainly before they can receive general absolution again. These, however, are disciplinary regulations and not theological obstacles. A person has truly been reconciled through this sacrament in this rite without individual confession and absolution.

2. *There must always be a proclamation of the Word of God.* In all three rites there is to be a Scripture reading. Even in individual confession the priest or the penitent should read some verses from Scripture before any sins are confessed. Either or both may share what these words mean to them personally. In the common penance celebrations the proclamation of the Word is often structured like the liturgy of the Word at Mass. The homily of the celebrant is usually centered on the mercy of God or our need for repentance.

3. *The rite must be visible, for such is the nature of liturgy.* The communal penance services are much more visible than the individual confessions. The very presence of a community praying together and confessing together expresses most visibly their solidarity in sin and their solidarity in grace. It is a most visible witness of mutual sorrow for how we have hurt one another and mutual forgiveness for that hurt. Another outward element of the rite is the fact the penitent is asked to express aloud a prayer of sorrow (act of contrition) as a visible sign of that repentance. The words of the priest absolving the penitent (or community present) are said aloud for the same reason. When individual absolution is given, the priest places his hands on the head of the penitent.

4. *It must be such that the people as a community can participate in it.* This aspect comes out much more clearly, of course, in the communal penitential services. There is the same type of singing, reading, praying, and dialogue as we see at Mass. Even in the individual rite, the penitent is called on to participate through Scripture reading and dialogue with the priest.

The introduction to the new rite of penance describes four basic aspects for the celebration of the sacrament: contrition, confession, satisfaction, and absolution.

On the part of the penitent the essential and therefore most important act is contrition. This is the underlying attitude that penitents must have before even approaching the sacrament of penance. They have decided to reject the former way of living out of love of Christ. The sorrow for sins arises out of a hatred for those actions which turned them away from God and out of a desire to draw closer to the one who made salvation possible.

It is out of that deep, heartfelt sorrow that *confession* takes place. The penitents acknowledge their reflection on that former way of life and confess those specific actions which brought about this alienation from God. (Lesser sins, though serious but not deadly, may also be appropriately confessed at this time.) It is healthy both psychologically and spiritually to confess those specific actions that drew the person away from God. In no other way does an audible dialogue with Christ come so meaningfully alive.

The *satisfaction,* or penance, is meant to be a re-entry into the mystery of salvation. Through their sins the penitents have separated themselves from the order of salvation. Although the contrition on their part assures reconciliation because of God's mercy and the saving deeds of Christ, this satisfaction is a gesture on their part, indicating their willingness to live the life of Christ. The rite suggests that there be some relationship between this sin committed and the satisfaction performed. Those who drink excessively might be called to do some fasting. Those guilty of racial bigotry might give some personal or material support to a civil rights group. Those involved in gossip might be asked to concentrate on affirming publicly the qualities of the person maligned.

The *absolution* is the visible sign of forgiveness on the part of the community. The priest absolves as the ordained spiritual leader of the Church which has authorized him to be its minister. The words of absolution express this dimension:

> God, the Father of mercies,
> through the death and resurrection of his Son
> has reconciled the world to himself
> and sent the Holy Spirit among us
> for the forgiveness of sins;
> through the ministry of the Church
> may God give you pardon and peace,
> and I absolve you from your sins
> in the name of the Father, and of the Son,†
> and of the Holy Spirit.

As the words indicate, God's pardon and peace come through the ministry of the Church. Because we believe that the Church is the sacrament of Christ, who is the sacrament of God, the absolution given by the priest in this sacrament is the visible sign of God's forgiveness. And the priest does it for us, the Church. We forgive; we are forgiven. Finally, it is an action involving the whole Trinity, Father, Son, and Holy Spirit. As the introduction to the rite says:

> In the sacrament of penance the Father receives the repentant son who
> comes back to him, Christ places the lost sheep on his shoulders and

brings it back to the sheepfold, and the Holy Spirit sanctifies this temple of God again or lives more fully within it. This is finally expressed in a renewed and more fervent sharing of the Lord's table, and there is a great banquet of God's Church over the son who has returned from afar (n. 6).

The sacrament itself must be seen more than merely in the ritual itself. It must be related to the whole life of a Christian. It is more than getting my sin forgiven. It involves healing a broken world, uniting a divided people, healing a wounded body. Again the introduction says:

In order that this sacrament of healing may truly achieve its purpose among Christ's faithful, it must take root in their whole lives and move them to more fervent service of God and neighbor (n. 6).

When I am open to receive the forgiveness of the sacrament, I also am to be a forgiver of others. It is often through experiencing the warmth of being forgiven that I am able to reach out and forgive others. If we are not a healing people, how can we be healed? If we are not a forgiving people, how can we be forgiven?

The sacrament of reconciliation serves the Christian community in many ways. It reconciles those who have been alienated through mortal sin. It helps those who, weakened through venial sins, seek to draw nearer to Christ. It helps the community as a whole to strengthen itself by healing wounds of division. It helps us to be sensitized to the evil of sin. It enables us to turn ourselves outward in trying to minister to the hurt and alienated. It helps us to come closer to Christ by forgiving others as Christ has forgiven us. In general, through this sacrament of reconciliation we enter more fully into the paschal mystery and live out more effectively the life of Christ begun through the sacraments of initiation.

QUESTIONS FOR REFLECTION

1. Have you ever experienced the hurt and alienation that Dolores did? Try to think of the "Alice" in your life who enabled you to open up. How did she do it? How did you feel?_____
_____
_____
_____
_____

2. Have you ever been in Alice's position? How did you respond? How did the other person respond?_____
_____
_____

3. Read again the parable of the Prodigal Son. Think of times in your life when you were the prodigal son . . . the forgiving father . . . the resentful brother.

4. Why is it important to stress this communal dimension of the sacrament of penance? How do you think the reformed rite of penance brings out this communal dimension?

ANOINTING OF THE SICK

The phone rings in the middle of the night. A groggy "hello" informs the caller that someone is at home. "Father, it's about time. I think mother is dying now. Could you come over?" So the priest grabs his ritual, oils, and coat and heads for the garage to drive over to the caller's home. As he arrives, he enters the house, and all the family says in a hushed tone to one another: "Father's here to give mother the last rites." They all quickly but quietly leave the room so that Father can be alone with their mother. The woman is so close to death that she cannot even respond, so the priest gives her conditional absolution and anoints each part of her body representing the different senses. The sacrament of extreme unction has been dutifully performed.

How we celebrate a sacrament says so much about our theology of sacrament. The very word "extreme unction" has an ominous ring to it. The sacrament was performed and viewed as a sacrament for the dying. Many priests will tell you that often people would not even want to see a priest in the hospital because of the association of the sacrament of extreme unction with death. This sacrament was almost seen as the *coup de grace.*

Yet sacraments are not to be seen as dead signs but living ones. Christ did not come to offer people death but life. It was in light of what the sacrament should convey that the Second Vatican Council reformed this sacrament. The first sign of this reform came with the name. It was changed from extreme unction to anointing of the sick. In promulgating this reformed rite of anointing, Pope Paul VI refers us to the letter of James:

> Is there anyone sick among you? He should ask for the presbyters of the church. They in turn are to pray over him, anointing him with oil in the Name [of the Lord]. This prayer uttered in faith will reclaim the one who is ill, and the Lord will restore him to health. If he has committed any sins, forgiveness will be his (Jas 5:14-15).

Anointing of the sick is then appropriately linked with penance as one of the sacraments of healing. It is an extension of the healing ministry exercised by Jesus while he was on earth.

Just as the community of Christians is the living sign of Christ today, the healing ministry of Christ takes place through the community of Christians called Church, carrying out this ministry through the sacrament of anointing. Like the other six sacraments, anointing of the sick is fundamentally a communal sacrament, not a private affair. Today if the priest in the above story were to come to the house to anoint the family's mother, he would be called while she was sick but long before she was dying. Instead of leaving the room the family would remain in the room to pray with the priest for their mother. The healing presence of Christ would be experienced through all of them coming together to pray.

A recent occurrence found in parish churches today is the communal rite of anointing. The sick and elderly are anointed in a parish celebration. Young and old come to pray for those to be anointed. Connected with this service are Scripture readings, a homily, and the communal prayers for the sick along with the anointing itself. Who may be included? How sick must one be? Anyone who has a serious illness is an appropriate recipient of Christ's healing presence. Although the elderly may not have any other infirmity except the weakness from old age, that would be cause in itself for being anointed, although advancement in years does not automatically mean debility.

People who are seriously ill are often challenged to the depths of their soul with some profound religious questions: Why me? Why is God allowing me to suffer like this? What is going to happen to my family? What is it like to die? It is at crisis moments such as a serious accident or illness that a person often begins asking deeply religious questions. This is when Christ often steps in to comfort, to soothe, and to become present to this person. Moments of conversion or rededication often occur because of such moments.

The sacrament of anointing is the celebration of the ministry of the Church in healing and caring for the sick. It is not just the ministry of the priests; it is the ministry of the whole Church. And it involves more than just anointing and praying. It involves the whole care and concern for those beset by illness. It is our giving witness to the fact that sickness is not simply a reality that is a natural part of life; rather, it is something which we must address. It is symbolic of our imperfect world. Yet it is an imperfection which we must try to perfect. It is an evil which we must try to eradicate with good, a brokenness which we must make whole.

If we are followers of Christ, we are each in our own way participants in the healing ministry.

QUESTIONS FOR REFLECTION

1. Think of the two phrases "extreme unction" and "anointing of the sick." What do you feel when you hear the two? Is there a difference?

2. What kind of healing are we seeking in this sacrament?

3. How does the communal nature of sacrament show in the anointing of the sick?

4. Does this sacrament tell us anything about our attitude as a people toward the sick and infirm?

5. How is this sacrament part of the ministry of persons other than priests?

Part Two

CATECHIST AS TEACHER

Unit One

DEVELOPMENT OF THE LESSON

PREFACE TO PART TWO

The first part of this book was directed at the catechist in formation. You have had the opportunity to review the message of Christ and his Church as an adult Christian. Hopefully, this has been more than an intellectual endeavor. It should have been an experiential journey of faith, that is, what was covered in the first part should have been viewed in light of your own experiences. The Scriptures show God revealing himself in so many ways, but always in terms of the experiences of the people to whom he was addressing himself.

As the first part indicated, catechesis should involve the same process as revelation. The catechist should take the learners through a journey of faith, trying to relate the life experience of the learners with the doctrine of Christ and his Church. If in the first part of this book you have undergone such a faith journey, then you have really experienced the process of catechesis. You can understand and appreciate an experiential approach to catechesis because you yourself have experienced it.

The second part of this book addresses the catechist as a teacher. You know the what of catechesis. You have experienced the how of catechesis. Now is the time to direct our attention to the skills, competencies, and aids that will enable the catechist to communicate the message effectively. In the first part of the book the catechist-instructor (master catechist) should have used a variety of methods, processes, and activities to help you come to a greater awareness of your faith. He or she should have modeled the methods of teaching which you should use when you teach. Your learners may be younger, but many of the principles for effective catechesis and teaching are the same. During this second part, we will reflect on some of the processes and activities which you have already experienced in this formation course.

Catechesis is much broader than teaching a classroom of children. It may involve adults. Even the catechesis of children may be connected with catechesis of parents. It may take place in a large hall or in one's home. It requires a lot of advance planning even before the session begins. It may call for a variety of teaching aids, sometimes including audio-visual equipment. These and many other things need to be looked at to make the catechist an effective teacher.

Things may appear to be considerably more involved than they were in the time of Jesus and the early Church. With the advent of computers, jets, television, and many forms of instant communication, we find ourselves living in a more complex age. In reviewing the Scriptures we see that revelation always came about through the experiences of the people. Were Jesus catechizing or evangelizing today, we have no doubt that the catechesis would reflect the complexities of a twentieth-century world.

1. EXPLORATION OF LESSON PLANNING

Any course on lesson planning and any text that has been written will include chapter after chapter explaining the various developments that take place before the finished product, a lesson plan, is completed.

To lessen the anxiety of the catechist in the area of lesson planning, let's look at lesson planning as we would in planning a trip. As a starting point for our trip we will need a map. This will allow us a degree of accuracy. If, for example, I wanted to travel from Boston, Massachusetts, to Little Rock, Arkansas, I first consider my reasons for the trip and what I would need for myself during the trip. I would have the car checked out to be certain that I had gas, oil, water, good tires, etc. I would have to be sure that I would have sufficient money to cover my expenses. Above all, I would need a well-charted map to know the miles to be traveled and the expected arrival time, and, most importantly, to ensure that I arrive at my destination and not in Orlando, Florida.

Lesson planning is like a trip. You need, first of all, to deal with the objective you hope to accomplish. Without an objective clearly thought out, you will end up probably never reaching your desired destination. Objectives in any lesson point the way, mark the route, and serve as checking points in your teaching situations. Perhaps you could underline or write the key words or ideas.

Think about those you are to visit: your learners. Learning is personal. If you don't know the learners in a personal way, how are you going to help them learn? We must remember that the students are unique individuals with varying abilities, attitudes, interests, and backgrounds.

One way of accomplishing this task is to have the students fill out a personal questionnaire. This can be as simple or complex as you might want for your purpose. Some questions might include: How many people are in your family? What are your two favorite television programs? What is your hobby? What is your favorite game? What is your birth date? This questionnaire could be kept in a file box or notebook for future reference. It serves as an invaluable way of getting to know your students.

This is one way. Each catechist may come up with other approaches. The way that most effectively does the job for you will be the best. To plan any lesson without considering the individuality of the learners is to neglect one of the most important aspects of teaching.

As you become familiar with the students as individuals, you are then able to begin the process of building community. This comes only after relationships have been developed. When this is accomplished in a Christian setting, you can be assured that truly Christian learning will take place.

Experience. What do I have to take with me? My suitcase will only hold so much, yet my closet is full. Learning experiences are very much like this. We have accumulated stores of materials and have a tendency to use them all. "Pack it in!" Any teacher's manual offers a variety of experiences. Let's look at the experiences in light of our stated objective. Does the experience help the objective become a reality? Since the experiences in any teacher's guide reflect a broad audience, it might not fit for use with your learners. If this should be the case, you are free to modify or substitute, but select your learning experience with your objective clearly understood.

How will your students relate to the learning experience? If telling stories does not work in your class, do not use story telling for the learning experience. If writing is difficult for your students, do not select an experience that would have the students write.

In considering the experience in light of the students, how are the students involved in the learning process? Does the experience lead to an active participation on the part of the learners?

When planning a trip it is of extreme importance to be practical. There are many points of interest between Boston and Little Rock. On the map I must mark the places where I would like to stop and list people whom I might want to visit. To do this I must consider time, interest, and money. In lesson planning I must do the same in a practical sense. If the parish setting for my class happens to be inner city with asphalt playgrounds, busy streets, and an absence of trees or grassy areas, it would not be practical to plan a nature walk. If I were in the Midwest, I would not plan a trip to the beach. If a projector is not available or if I am unable to operate one, I would not schedule a film for part of the lesson. Catechists must approach their teaching situation from a practical point of view. This will necessitate creatively changing the recommended learning experience to fit the uniqueness of their situation.

Finally, as I prepare for my trip, I should reflect on whether or not I am comfortable about it. In a small city in Ohio there is a well-known snake farm. The farm offers guided tours at reasonable prices and advertises the largest boa constrictor in captivity. It may sound very attractive to some, but not if one is terrified of snakes. If this were the case, it would not be advisable to make this stop.

In lesson planning the catechist has to be comfortable with the plan. Mime, pantomime, and role-playing are all effective vehicles for learning if the catechist is comfortable with these methods. If the catechist is uncomfortable, then the vehicle can be devastating. Catechists must always know that what is planned is within their ability to carry it out.

Below is a developed lesson plan. Each step in the preparation is vital to successful teaching. This is only one of a variety of existing models that can be used. If you are using a particular textbook in your catechetical program, your teacher's manual might possibly use a different model for lesson planning. Whatever is suggested may be used. Lesson planning is one sure way of being certain that you are effectively presenting the materials.

MODEL LESSON PLAN

1. LESSON THEME: (in a textbook, usually the title of the lesson) Let Us Give Thanks (coming together for worship)

How does the lesson appear to fit the unit? The unit deals with the Church. This particular lesson deals with the students' understanding of coming together for the eucharistic celebration.

How does it relate to the last lesson? We worked on the Church as the people of God. In this lesson we will see the people of God gathering to participate in a communal celebration.

2. LESSON OBJECTIVE: What particular point do you want to get across in regard to the message?

What do I want the class to learn? To lead the students to a deeper awareness that God's people form a family and that they assemble together as a family for the action of worship.

What attitudes and understandings do I hope to build? An appreciation of their role as participants in the action of worship.

3. PERSONAL LEARNING RESOURCES:

Student experience: The students are able to recall most clearly those sacramental experiences that they have participated in. They are able to relate to their first reception of the Eucharist or the marriage of a brother or sister. They especially recall when their own involvement itself was the very reason for the celebration.

My experience: I in fact have learned to live out the celebration in my daily life through action.

4. TEACHING METHODS (Check the ones needed)

____game	____filmstrip	____storytelling
____visitor	____record	____lecture
____art activity	____tape recording	____student research
____writing	____reading	____music activity
____role playing	____discussion	____dramatization
____other		____group project

5. TEACHING MATERIALS:

Materials I need: Poster paper, marking pens, masking tape, slides, slide projector, extension cord, posters.

Materials students need: Books, poster paper, marking pens.

6. PROCEDURE: How will I get students interested?

1. Discuss the worshiping community as a sign of faith and love.

2. Ask the students for a definition of sign. (A sign is something that tells us about something else.)

3. Show slides of signs that students are familiar with, e.g., stop signs, billboards, directional signs.

4. Have the students make signs that show people as signs, e.g., people gathering for a family dinner, watching a sports event, greeting people, etc.

5. Discuss the worshiping community as sign. Explain how the gathering of people for worship is a sign of their belief in the risen Christ and their love for him. It is a sign of their willingness to come together to hear God's Word and to share in the Eucharist. It is a sign of their being joined with the risen Christ in faith and love.

6. Discuss how the worshiping community is a sign for others that we have and share love for one another and for all people.

7. Using their posters have each student write a brief prayer. This is to be shared in the closing prayer service using as their theme that each of us is a sign to others.

7. HOW DID I DO?

Did the students seem to learn? Did they enjoy the class? Did I enjoy the class? How could I have improved the class?

You are ready to start your trip. Regardless of the detours (varying approaches to lesson plans) you are prepared to start feeling confident and comfortable.

Don't forget the *keys,* or the trip will never get under way.

2. MODELS OF LESSON PLANS

MODEL 1

Aim. The aim of the lesson consists in the doctrine to be presented as well as the students' response that is expected. In preparing the aim of the lesson catechists know that it will give direction and that they have considered the psychological, social, and spiritual interests of the students.

Prayer. The catechist is free to place the prayer where it will be most appropriate to the lesson. The prayer should always be centered on the *message* that is being given. Use a variety of prayer experiences, either formal or informal (spontaneous). Allow the students to develop their own prayer and form.

Preparation. This is laying the groundwork for the lesson. It serves as the orientation time, enabling the catechist to determine what the students already know about the material to be presented, to gain the students' attention, and to motivate them in the learning experience. The catechist might do this by asking a few questions relevant to the subject matter. Since learning is relational, the catechist in the preparation section should encourage the students to relate to the subject matter from other material they already know or from their ability to recall an experience that would furnish background material for the subject.

The area of the lesson plan called preparation is of key importance to the catechist. This is where one is most easily able to capture the attention and interest of the students. It is the motivational aspect of the lesson.

Presentation. The message that is to be presented is done at this time by the catechist. Attention must be paid by the catechist to the learners' attention span. Most often we find the catechist "over-talking" for the ability of the learner. In this area "over-talking" creates "over-kill," and the result in the lesson is failure. Know what you want to do, and select any of a variety of ways to assist you in the presentation, e.g., film, filmstrip, flannel-board, story telling, concrete objects, etc. In your presentation simplicity and clarity should be your guide.

Explanation. The catechist will take concrete examples or situations used in the presentation and apply it to the message that was presented to make it clearer to the student. The explanation must be logical, interesting, and clear. Explanation often overlaps with presentation; therefore, the catechist might develop this section with the presentation. One must clearly see, however, that one moves from material that is known to material you want to present that is new (unknown). The explanation allows for making comparison, analyzing, scrutinizing, and showing relationships.

Application. Here the catechist takes the message and enables the students to see the relationship between the message and their lives. It motivates them to direct their conduct according to the truths they have learned. This may be done when the catechist gives a practical explanation, or it might include the students by the presentation of questions, problem solving, or concrete examples shared by the students.

Assimilation. This part of the lesson plan enables the message to become part of us. It is that time when the catechist helps the students to digest and accept the message as their very own. It is no longer unknown material; rather through assimilation it becomes intellectual knowledge.

Summarization. Looking at the message as it has been presented, explained, and analyzed, the catechist now synthesizes and summarizes the message. This can be done by having the students review their understanding of the message either orally or in writing.

MODEL 2

(W. H. Sadlier, Inc., Lord of Life Program, 1978. The Lord of Life program is a life centered approach to catechesis consisting of three movements: life experience, faith development, and faith response.)

I. *Life Experience* This includes personal experience, group experience, and reflection. A basic life experience is brought into focus by shared reflection. This is done in a class through an initial group activity which leads to the next step, faith development.

II. *Faith Development.* This section includes Scripture, Church teachings, and liturgy adapted to the needs and understanding of the group. This in turn calls for the next step, faith response.

III. *Faith Response.* This section would include understanding, appreciation, prayer, and service. The faith response would be both personal and communal. The personal responses of understanding, appreciation, and prayer can and do take place anytime during the process. The communal responses, celebration of our faith in prayer and service, ought to be planned and should aim at conversion or renewal of *life* in response to God, the Lord of life.

MODEL 3

(Silver Burdett Company, Religious Education Program, 1977)

Stage 1, Exploring Life. This section entails exploring some segments of the students' life experience. The strategy aims at stimulating thought, reflection, and questions. It challenges and invites one to go deeper into one's experience and religious heritage.

Stage 2. Sharing Tradition. This section entails sharing a related aspect of Christian tradition. What has been learned through exploration or reflection is meant to be shared with others who take part in the learning experience. Like exploring, sharing also takes place in terms of life and tradition. Sharing, in turn, is an important stimulus to individual and group reflection.

Stage 3. Integration of Life and Tradition. This section entails prayer. Since faith is primarily a relationship of trust in and love of God, prayer is absolutely critical to learning. Genuine Christian prayer arises out of daily experiences and is nourished on the rich heritage of Christian spirituality. Praying flows from exploring and sharing and is a further dimension of each.

MODEL 4

(Paulist Press, Come to the Father Program, 1969)

1. *The Recall of a Universal Human Experience.* Open the class itself with an experience meaningful to the students. Draw to their attention an experience that they live regularly at home, in class, with friends, etc. Broaden this experience with the help of added facts, witnesses, etc. The catechist must find ways and means to make the experience come alive for the learners.

2. *Recall Preceding Lesson.* This period of time should provide for the catechist an opportunity to check whether the past lesson has been assimilated by the student. It allows the students to connect what they know and what is to be learned.

3. *The Human Experience in Its Christian Dimension.* During the lessons devoted to reliving and examining the human experience, the children should begin to see its depth and vital significance. They are invited to pursue their understanding or "reading" of the experience in greater depth, guided by God's Word.

This is further enhanced by presenting the witness of Christians, a Gospel word or deed, or a liturgical sign. Drawing light from the witness of fellow Christians, the words of the Gospel and liturgical signs, the students will be enabled "to read" for themselves the human experiences taken from their own lives and proposed for their reflection. They will become more capable of reading these experiences as signs of the Lord's presence and action in their lives.

4. *Discussion.*

A. *Development.* Here is where catechists must be able to relinquish their authority and attempt to understand and use to full advantage the students' questions, answers, and points of interest.

B. *The Students' Questions.* This development of questions would be in relationship to the age of readiness and ability to understand of the learner. Answers to questions for the most part should be found by the learners. This can provide for individual or group research. At times the answers to questions will be found. Questions relating to the life of faith are not always easily understood. Catechists should not be afraid to take their place with the learners on the level of faith. This will allow the students to see that catechists also believe in God's Word without fully understanding its mystery.

5. *Activities.* "Activities are a pedagogical procedure to help the interiorization of those being catechized." The activities used in the program may be placed into three categories.

A. *Research Activities:* The learners will be asked to carry out research projects using the Gospel, parish bulletins, or missals. They will be able to finish the documentary research by consulting dictionaries, other classroom manuals, the newspapers, etc.

B. *Interiorizing Activities:* Activities that are planned to help the student in their spiritual understanding of the Gospel message and to stimulate faith, hope, or charity, which is specifically Christian activity. These activities may be in the forms of discussion, drawings, composition, making up of prayer cards, team study of text, etc.

C. *Integrating Activities:* These activities aim to deepen the students' faith as it is lived today so that they may participate fully in liturgical life, know present-day life of Christians better, and deepen their awareness of the meaning of prayer. Among these activities we should place celebrations, the making of prayer cards, research projects on the Christian life, documents reporting the witness given by Christians of our time, and the preparation of bulletin boards.

D. *Their Realization.* These activities can be carried out (1) individually or (2) collectively in the case of panels made by teams, preparation for a celebration, the study of a text, etc. Care should be taken to balance these two types of activity. On the one hand, individual work allows students to reflect personally and interiorize the message at their own pace. On the other hand, collective work or teamwork allows a lot more ideas. Teamwork has the advantage of helping the slower student intellectually and those who are more superficial in their reflection.

Whatever text you are using, whatever way you develop your lesson plan, it will be personal to you the catechist. The greatest message you have for the learners is not the text. What is of utmost importance to the learners is *you.* A well-thought-out, planned approach of sharing your faith with others takes place through the development of your lesson plan. It enables you to be free in expressing yourself and serves only to assure you that what you wanted to accomplish has been done.

3. EXPERIENCE OF THE CATECHIST VERSUS THE STUDENT

If the experiences we share with students are to be meaningful, they must be told within the range of the students' ability to understand. We must rethink the words being used so that they reach the students and convey the right concept. We want it to make sense to the learner, whether child or adult. We must project ourselves into the world of the students, see things from the perspective of their mind's eye, speak in terms of their limited experience, and anticipate their mental reactions. If we permit the opportunity to retell or illustrate by drawing a story we have shared, we may be surprised at the insight we can gain into the working of their minds.

A first grade teacher was explaining to her class a rather vivid description of the Blessed Mother's bringing the Messiah into the world. This teacher gave some background on the stable where Jesus was born and said that it was located in Bethlehem, a city in the Holy Land. Then she had the students retell the story. One young boy did a rather complete job. In addition, he added to the story by sharing with the class that his grandparents were making a trip to the Holy Land over the summer vacation. He was very excited about this story and was going to ask his grandmother to stop by and visit with Mary. The first grade student had not yet acquired any sense of history. The world of a first grader is quite small and ego-centered. The child did not have the ability to comprehend that Mary lived many centuries ago. To him, it was all part of his world, the world of here and now.

One must be aware of who the students are. In presenting God the Father as one who loves us and cares for us, very often catechists will use the example of family. They will talk about fathers, mothers, brothers, sisters, or grandparents. In today's society one must be certain to whom one is talking. In many family situations there is not a good image of loving fathers and mothers. To present God indiscriminately in this type of image has often created a reverse effect on some students. We must always look to the students' experience and be extremely sensitive and prudent in this area.

We must also keep in mind when we are teaching the young that we have lived many more years than the students with whom we are working. During the years of our life we have stored a wealth of experiences. Our students have not lived the same number of years; therefore, their experiences are limited. Those who lived through the 1940's experienced World War II, food and gas rationing, the Marshall Plan, and the revolution in China. Those living in the 1950's experienced the Korean War, the Supreme Court decision outlawing segregation in public schools, the defiance of integration at Central High School in Little Rock, and the beginning of the space era with the Russian satellite Sputnik. Those in the 1960's experienced the space race to the moon, the Kennedy assassination, Martin Luther King and civil rights, the Vietnam War, draft resistance, and the war on poverty. In general, the students who are in catechetical classes are too young to have lived through this part of history. It does not reflect their experience. It is past history and certainly not part of the world scene as they are experiencing it. Catechists must be capable of entering into the experience of the learner and becoming familiar with it. They must strive for an appreciation and understanding of what is happening in the lives of the learners. Listening to their music, watching their programs and films, and reading their literature can be of great help in trying to catechize out of their everyday experiences.

The cultural and ethnic origins of people significantly color their experience. We find that in a country as multi-cultural as ours, there is a variety of persons living, working, caring, and sharing together. If the catechist is to meet the learner where the learner is, it is necessary to have some background on who the students are and where they come from. This might entail some knowledge of the experience of black Americans or Hispanics or whatever group of people comprise the learners. Without this appreciation of the experience of the learners, we tend to lose the beauty, richness, and gift that can be gained from them.

A group of dedicated, sincere individuals had chosen for their ministry to the Church the catechesis of youths in detention facilities (juvenile halls and camps). They had worked for a number of years in the detention program, isolated from diocesan catechetical programs. A sister was assigned by the diocese to be responsible for the catechesis of youths in detention. She called a meeting of the volunteer catechists to introduce herself and to find out how the program was operating. Because he was involved in the program longer than the rest, one particular man became the spokesperson for the group. When the sister asked about the teaching situation, he quickly informed her that "these kids are dangerous." He rattled off a rapid run-down of the kinds of incidents that put the youths in a detention facility. He concluded by informing her that the catechists barely had time to get across the most important message. "What message is that?" was the sister's response. Utterly amazed that a sister should even have to ask such a question, he arrogantly replied: "These kids don't understand that they are on their way to hell if they don't mend their ways. We have to get that across to them."

To a group of youths who had experienced nothing but rejection and failure, eternal damnation was the last thing they needed to hear. It only magnified the deep guilt feelings they already had. Needless to say, since that first meeting there have been many changes in the personnel now working with these youths. If only these catechists had had an appreciation of the experience of their learners, how much better would the catechists have been able to deal with the situation! These people were dedicated and well intentioned but totally lacking any understanding of the experience of the young person.

To become proclaimers of the "good news," each of us must be able to relate to the audience we are addressing. If our message is beyond our learners' ability to understand or is totally alien to their personal experience, it only becomes another piece of "bad news." The catechist has experiences that are valid and helpful in their ministry. These experiences can be used wherever they meet the needs of the group of learners. However, they should never be used when they are misunderstood or beyond the ability of the group of learners to relate to. The catechist must look at the group, try to understand their experience, and, in light of that experience, present a message that will become intelligible and relevant to the learner.

QUESTIONS FOR REFLECTION

1. Look at the learners or potential learners at the age level or situation in which you are or will be teaching. What are the life experiences they as a group will have gone through?

2. Look at your own life experience when you were at the age of your learners. How has society presented them with a different life experience? _____
_____
_____
_____
_____

3. Look at the textbook with which you will be working. How does its doctrinal content meet the religious readiness of your learners? _____
_____
_____
_____
_____

4. APPLICATION OF EXPERIENCE TO MESSAGE

In a learning situation catechists must be careful to apply the experience of the student to the message. The message is what we want to share with the student. It can be most effectively understood when presented in light of the student's experience. To work with the message portion of the lesson without taking into account the experience of the learners quite often creates in them boredom, confusion, and disinterest. In the application of experience to the message, the catechist has a responsibility to design creatively a variety of ways to achieve the desired result.

In the chapter on revelation we saw how God revealed himself through the experience of the people to whom he was communicating. He took into account culture, education, customs, and political situations. Jesus likewise used the everyday experience of his audience. He always kept in mind the views, prejudices, vocabulary, interest, and general background of his learners. To those who were tillers of the soil, Jesus spoke simply of seeds, sower, wheat and weeds; to the fishermen he spoke of nets, fish, and empty and filled nets; to the doctors of the law, he discussed and argued the Scriptures. Jesus taught by applying the experience of the learners to the message he wanted to impart. By means of many such parables he taught them the message in a way they could understand (Mk 4:33).

God's process of revelation and Jesus' way of teaching and preaching should be the way for the catechist. If, for example, we were to present the message of the Sermon on the Mount to the learners, we would first begin by exploring with the students situations with which they are familiar: the hungry being fed, the poor being clothed, the oppressed being set free. We might begin by using newspapers; the students would search there for articles that would correlate. Another way to begin might be to have the students write a paragraph that would tell where they have seen any of these things being done. Or we might ask the class if any of them would like to share an experience that would give insight on one of the examples. Their experience would be the preparation for the presentation of the message. The learners would have a greater level of interest because they would be able to see their involvement related to the message.

Virtually any catechetical textbook in use today and considered acceptable by most professional religious educators has been prepared to assist the catechist in applying the learners' experience to the message. It has been the experience of catechists that consideration of the experience of the learners is of prime importance if learning is to happen.

Another example would be in the preparation of students for the reception of First Eucharist. We find the textbooks talking about special family meals, e.g., Thanksgiving, birthdays, etc. Primary students are capable of relating these experiences to their own lives. From their experience we are then able to share an understanding of the Eucharist as a special meal where we encounter Jesus and are nourished by him. Because of the primary children's limited experience and inability to understand abstract concepts, the catechist must use language that is intelligible to them.

For learners to understand, whether adult or child, it is necessary for them to depend on some previous experience. To share an experience that is beyond their ability to comprehend would be meaningless. To choose an experience that is totally irrelevant to a person's everyday life reduces catechesis to an exercise in theology. It will have little or no connection with anything the learner knows or cares about. It will be a useless venture, for there is no connection between religion and life. A person will be unable to interpret new situations and new experiences in light of the message. The message is the essence of the lesson. Therefore, to share the message, it is of utmost importance that catechists share the message in light of the learners' experience. Catechesis becomes a means of God's revelation, and the catechist is God's living instrument.

QUESTIONS FOR REFLECTION

Take the following themes: God loves us; God became a human being; Church is the people of God.

1. How would your experience lead to the development of each of these themes?_____
_____
_____
_____
_____

2. How would the experience of your learners lead to the development of each of these themes?

Unit Two

THE LEARNING SITUATION

1. A LOOK AT THE LEARNERS

As catechists we must center our planning of any lesson on the learners. Who are they? Where do they come from? Why are they here? These are but a few of the questions we need to ask ourselves as we ponder the material to be presented. In Unit V of the first part of this book we identified the stages of growth and readiness for the message. Take a look now at the grade level you are working with. After you have done that, you are ready to answer the following three questions.

Who are they? Your learners are individuals, unique and special to you. They are eager to learn, provided that the experience is within their ability to comprehend. Due to the diverse families to which each of them belongs, they have a broad range of religious experiences that have been integrated within them, making them who they are. As catechists we are yet another experience for the student. We can become a major formative influence more by who we are than by what we teach. The catechist is responsible for fostering an atmosphere of security and love within the learners. All learning processes therefore must be concerned with who the learners are. A catechist must look at their needs and experiences and center the learning process around them. The catechist must help the learners develop their creative talents in accordance with their abilities.

Where do they come from? In the majority of situations your learners come from a particular parish community. The catechist is the best source of knowing what that community is like. If your parish community is a "filling station" where the members arrive each Sunday to get their tanks filled for the week, be assured that this is where they come from. Perhaps they live on the fringe community and look at catechetical programs as merely a means of obtaining sacraments. Accept it as a reality. It is. There are many persons who fit into this category. And many of them have been destroyed by well-intentioned catechists who become discouraged by the students' ignorance of their religion.

Another model is the parish community that involves the people, provides for their active involvement, and welcomes all people, not just selected cliques. Although this model is not often prevalent, it stands the best chance of providing a willingness to enter into the formation process of building one's faith. Such a community has reached out to the alienated and made them feel welcome and a part of the parish. There are many other models besides these few. It becomes the task of the catechist to deal with any model and to meet the learners from wherever they may come. You must greet them and make them your own. By your caring for them and your sharing of yourself, you show each person that you truly have been called to share in the work of Jesus through this catechetical ministry.

Why are they here? The reasons why they are here are many: some good, some not so good. If the reasons are not the noblest, it is often the result of the parents' and/or the learners' lack of understanding of what catechesis is all about. The fact, however, remains: the students are here. A catechist with concern for the students is the key to keeping them. To keep them it is crucial how catechists go about building a loving Christian atmosphere in the learning situation, how they get to know their students, how they involve the students in what they are going to learn, how that learning takes place, and how they enable friendships to be developed.

Stop for a moment and think about yourself and your involvements. You belong to various communities. First you are a member of your family community. Then you belong to a community at work. You belong to various clubs or organizations, either social or civic. As you think about these different communities, you may find that some have more meaning to you than others. There are some in which you really enjoy participating. There are others to which you barely belong. You make many excuses to avoid attending their meetings or functions. What seems to be the difference? The group that interests you the most is the group that cares about you. It is the group where people are involved and where you want to be part of that involvement. It is the place where you feel secure and part of what is happening.

Whether child or adult, each of us comes from a variety of experiences. Some of our experiences are more positive than others. If as catechists we really work at getting to know regarding our learners *who they are, where they come from,* and *why they are here,* we will develop a clearer understanding as to what we must do in the learning process. We will be able to build an atmosphere of trust where the learners know that they are cared for, welcomed, wanted, and secure. It is only in this kind of setting that learning is possible. We will then have learners who are contented and looking forward to their time together as a learning community.

QUESTIONS FOR REFLECTION

1. Take a look at your learners. Make a statement about their diversity and similarities.

2. What motivated them to come to your class in the first place?

3. How will you as a catechist meet the needs of such a group of learners?

2. ASSESSMENT OF NEEDS

Almost all of us know what a missionary is. A missionary is one sent out to preach the Word of God to people who are not Christians. We have heard many stories from the pulpit by missionaries making appeals for help. These people have touched far-distant countries living under adverse conditions and performing a variety of activities in service of the people. Before being sent to these far-off lands, missionaries are usually trained in medicine, farming, plumbing, engineering, and carpentry. Most of their work involves more practical service than spiritual and religious instruction.

The Missionaries of Charity, founded by Mother Teresa of Calcutta, spend only a fraction of their time preaching about Christ. They never go out on mission without carrying some food along. Why? Because the most pressing need of these people is food for survival. Until the most immediate needs are met, a person seeks no other need.

The psychologist, Abraham Maslow, held that human motivation can be related to almost every aspect of individual and social life. He sees the human being

165

as an integrated whole, and therefore the whole person is motivated, not just a part. His basic concept is that the human being is motivated by a number of basic needs which are species-wide, apparently unchanging, and genetic or instinctual in origin. These needs transcend culture and race, and they are both physiological and psychological.

According to Maslow, the human being is always motivated by the desire to satisfy needs. When one need is satisfied, another one arises. He sees a hierarchy of needs beginning with the most basic and going up to the most lofty and ideal. It is only when the lower needs are satisfied that a person is motivated to feel loftier needs. The most basic and most powerful needs are those necessary for physical survival: needs for food, liquid, shelter, sex, sleep, and oxygen. If a person has no food, other needs for affirmation or self-esteem will be suppressed until hunger has been satisfied.

Once these physiological needs are met, a person has certain safety needs. This is especially evident in a child in need of the security of home and family. Children coming from unstable homes or uncaring parents are extremely insecure and can pose real discipline problems. Neurotic adults are often people who have not satisfied these particular needs. It is then important that in a learning session catechists be sensitive to fulfilling this safety need in their students. Favoritism, inconsistency in discipline, frequent absences, and poorly prepared lessons create a climate detrimental to this need for safety or security.

Once these physiological and safety needs have been met, there arise the needs for belonging and love. A person wants to be part of the group and desires close relationships of friendship and intimacy. Studies have shown this deep need for love even among babies.

Maslow saw two types of esteem needs. One is self-respect and the other is the esteem from others. If people do not have a positive image of themselves, it is difficult for growth to take place. But that self-respect needs to be coupled with the affirmation from others. No matter how self-confident and self-assured a person may appear, support and affirmation is needed and appreciated. This moves a person onward and upward in growth as an integrated individual.

Once these lower needs have been satisfied, we are no longer just struggling along. We have acquired a certain happiness and well-being. Now there arise higher and more spiritual needs. Our quest now is to grow further into a self-actualized person. The growth needs are closely interrelated, virtually impossible to separate, and not placed in any particular hierarchical order. Maslow listed fourteen values which a person feels need for and called them "Being-values": wholeness, perfection, completion, justice, aliveness, richness, simplicity, beauty, goodness, uniqueness, effortlessness, playfulness, truth (honesty), and self-sufficiency.

Whether you accept Maslow's theory completely or not, it is good to keep in mind this hierarchy of needs. A catechist's failure to meet the perceived needs of learners may be due to failure in satisfying some of the more basic needs.

Needs assessment of the learners is essential to any teacher. In most catechetical situations, the more fundamental needs are usually taken care of. But it is important that the catechist not assume too much. What a catechist sees as a need for the learners may be something that the learners are not even aware of. For example, the catechist may feel that it is important for the learners to understand the mystery of the Holy Trinity. However, if the learners have not even come to know Jesus as man and as God and developed a relationship with him, if they have not come to an appreciation of the work of God in creation and in the history of mankind, if they have not seen the working of the Holy Spirit both in the Scriptures and in their lives, they will not feel the need to learn about the mystery of the Trinity. What the catechist perceives as a need for the learners must flow out of the felt needs of the learners.

I must be motivated to learn. I must *want* to learn. This is known as a "felt need." But what a learner wants may not necessarily be what the learner really needs to learn. What the learner really needs to learn is known as a "real need." To be an effective teacher, the catechist needs to determine both felt needs and real needs. The objective is to satisfy the real needs. This is done most effectively by satisfying the felt needs of the learners in order to motivate them to fulfill the real need.

If you are teaching children on the elementary or junior high level, generally the textbooks have already assessed the needs according to the different age levels. A great deal of study has been done to determine what are the needs of children at those age levels in their growth as Christians. A look at scope-and-sequence charts shows at a glance how these curricula have been developed. These are the real needs which you wish to meet. However, depending on the group of learners, there are many different ways of meeting those needs. Often even their real needs may vary. If the learners of the fifth grade, for example, are beginning religious instruction for the first time, their needs will be more fundamental than a group of learners who are in their fifth, sixth, or seventh year of catechesis. They may be in the same grade and of the same age, but have vastly different needs.

Where the assessment of felt needs is of utmost importance is in adolescent and adult catechesis. By that time the learners are only coming if they really want to. No longer is attendance based on simply the parents' desire that they go. A catechist must know what they are looking for to satisfy themselves. In light of that the catechist designs a course. Some learners are interested in Scripture, but not all. Some are interested in spirituality, but not all. Some are interested in conscience formation, but not all. At these age levels, unless catechists make a careful assessment of the felt and real needs of their learners, effective catechesis will not take place.

QUESTIONS FOR REFLECTION

1. What are the felt needs of your learners?_____
_____
_____
_____
_____

2. What are the needs of your learners according to your assessment?_____
_____
_____
_____
_____

3. TECHNIQUES FOR MOTIVATION

The success or failure of catechists depends to a great extent on their ability to motivate the students in the learning process. Simply stated, this means developing within the learners the desire they must have for their own best interests as well as the best interests of society. To accomplish this, desired goals must be set, and the learners' behavior must be directed to attaining the goals.

We have often heard people trying to determine the cause of a particular action by an individual. Detectives are always looking for the motive to assist them in solving the case. Motive is the inner drive proceeding from the rational faculties of intellect and will which allows a person to act or not to act, or to act in one way rather than another. This action is expressed in outward behavior.

Motivation is the factor that enables us to direct an individual toward the attainment of a particular goal. It is the opportunity to stimulate or develop interest in a particular goal where little or no interest previously existed.

Take any group of students involved in a catechetical program. They each have different motives for being present. Catechists are called to look into these motives in order to determine what motivational techniques they will need to use for learning to take place.

Jim is eleven years old. His dad was the top baseball player on the high school team, and from the time Jim was a few weeks old, his dad just knew that Jim was going to follow in the "old man's footsteps." But unfortunately Jim was not good at baseball. He lacked the coordination necessary to excel in the sport. Unable to recognize the child's inability to excel in that sport, Jim's father kept him in Little League activities. Jim became angry, sullen, and rebellious. During his physical education classes at school, the coach had a real behavioral problem with him. He caused trouble in any team activity and resented any help offered by the coach. In talking with Jim one day, the coach was able to determine the motives behind Jim's actions. Together they developed goals that Jim could reasonably achieve. The anger, sullenness, and rebellion soon disappeared, and Jim became an eager learner.

Susan is in the eighth grade. She was enrolled in the parish catechetical program because her parents knew it was about time for her to receive the sacrament of confirmation. She had not been to a CCD class since second grade when she made her first confession and First Communion. During the next six years Susan and her mother would occasionally attend Mass. For the most part, however, they would sleep in on Sunday. It was the only day the family had to rest. Susan's dad did not go to church at all. He had lawns to mow, cars to wash, and things to repair, and besides, as he said, God knew that he was busy.

Susan had little background, if any, when she entered the class. The material in class was "Greek" to her. For the first four weeks she sat through the class bored, embarrassed, and wondering why she had to be there. She was certainly a stranger to the group and did not know any of the other students.

The catechist observed Susan's lack of participation and boredom. In the fourth week of class he asked Susan to remain after class so that he might talk with her. Discovering Susan's problem (which is not unique), the catechist explored with her some alternatives to the situation. A conference with Susan, her parents, and the catechist was arranged. Both Susan and her family were encouraged by the catechist's interest in them as a family.

The catechist encouraged Susan's parents to join a group of adults who met each week at the church for discussion on "Changes in the Church." Understanding the problem enabled him to motivate both parents and child to begin actively participating in the Church.

Providing choices, attitudes, and ideals is what motivation is about. To motivate the students, the catechist must understand them. How do they view religion, Jesus or the Church? What is their ambition, hobby, selection of reading material, film, or television program, etc. What attitudes have they formed in the areas of morals and social justice? All of these are significant factors in the students' development toward adulthood.

The catechist then must be a person who is in touch with those experiences that are meaningful in the life of the students. Using their experiences can often be the springboard for fruitful discussion and successful catecheis.

In order to be a motivator as a catechist, you must first be reachable to the learners. If they feel an atmosphere of acceptance on your part, they will feel comfortable with you and secure in communicating honestly. There must be a willingness on your part to share openly your inner self with your students. You must be sensitive to their needs, show a positive attitude toward life, and be able to stir the imagination that will create a desire in them to find meaning and direction in their lives.

Once you understand your students, formulate goals that will respond to their needs. Be certain that the goals are expressed clearly and are understood by the students. Include them in the formulation of the goals. Evaluate the goals periodically to measure the success of the group in their attainment of them.

As a catechist you have the responsibility of making the students feel that they belong to the group. Show that you recognize them by calling them by name, speaking to them whenever and wherever you see them, commending their work, and displaying good work. Show that you care for them by your willingness to work with them, by being friendly in your approach, by thanking them for their efforts, and by showing them that you understand them. Allow them to be responsible. Provide situations that will allow each student to succeed according to each one's capabilities.

These are just a few ideas of how to motivate the learners. In general, to enable learning to take place, the students must want to learn, and the catechist must want them to learn something they don't already know. The catechist believes that the students need to know something new. When a student wants to learn something, that is called a "felt need." When the catechist finds out that the student does not know something, e.g. a particular doctrine or religious teaching, that lack on the student's part is a "real need." The end of learning is to fulfill that real need. But the catechist must begin with the felt need. It is through the felt need that catechists motivate their learners to attain that real need.

The key then to motivation is to know the learners, really understand where they are coming from, and then approach one's lesson in a way that will be relevant to them.

QUESTIONS FOR REFLECTION

1. Looking at the felt and real needs of the last section, how do you plan to satisfy the needs of your learners?_____
_____
_____
_____
_____

2. Why do you feel this would be an effective motivation in the learning process?_____
_____
_____
_____
_____

4. COPING WITH THE STUDENTS

In any learning situation, a catechist finds a variety of people in the group. A "typical" or homogenous group just does not exist. Many learners are extremely well motivated and participate for the right reasons. Others are in attendance because of the pressure of others, e.g. parents, and some are there quite often because of a particular moment in their life, e.g., baptism, confirmation, First Eucharist, or first penance.

To enable learning to take place, one must first have an interested audience. The catechist who makes an assumption that each learner in the group is present, eager to learn, and looking forward to class will rapidly recognize that the assumption is inaccurate.

If you as a catechist are unable to recognize the variety of persons and their individual reasons for being in the group, you are already in trouble. Each session with the learners will increase both your frustration and that of your students, and everyone will tend to become discouraged, angry, and often depressed at the thought of the next session. "Battle fatigue" has set in, with those involved no longer able to cope. In such a situation catechists begin to look for other areas of ministry in the Church while the students look for any reason to be absent or, better yet, to quit. The picture is sad, dismal, and seemingly hopeless, but the situation is real. Catechetical programs throughout the country have experienced it. What is the solution?

Foolproof solutions for this situation are not easy. There must be a great deal of willingness on the part of catechists to work through the variety of problems that created the situation. It is possible to offer assistance to catechists that can go a long way toward helping them to overcome the barriers that they may have encountered in their attempts to share God's love with their students.

Think of the different kinds of students that comprise a class. Some of the students have been placed in the class because they have reached a "golden age," i.e., that time in their life when they are to receive one of the sacraments. Looking at these students, we tend to find that they come from homes where there is a half-hearted or misunderstood approach to religion. Others are in the class because of a great pressure on the part of their parents.. This pressure has created for these students fear of not excelling or of meeting expectations that they are not sufficiently mature enough to achieve. Some students are at that level of maturity where they look at the catechist as an adult authority figure, and the result is rebellion. Many others have experienced learning problems in school. These children often tend to view themselves as failures. Catechetical classes to such children are often just another area in which they will fail.

In summary, one must look at all the possible situations. What is the home life of each student? How does each student relate to other members of the group? How does each student relate to the catechist? Is every student capable of understanding the religious content? Does each student have the necessary mentality to feel secure in participating in the class?

Each catechist must pray to God for the gifts of patience and insight—patience to realize that time is of great importance. A seed that is planted takes time to germinate. It requires great care, water, sun, and the nourishment of the soil. It rarely, if ever, blooms in front of our eyes but rather in its own time. Without our caring for it, it will surely die. Patience is required if we are to see it grow and bear fruit. Insight is needed to be able to understand and be capable of recognizing the uniqueness of each individual. It requires an appreciation of what stage of readiness the learner is prepared for. It demands the ability to know that, handled in the correct way, the learner wants to know God and to develop an ever-deepening relationship with the Father.

While you are in the midst of a learning session and you perceive a problem arising, ask the individual to see you after the session. An opportunity to talk freely with the learner in a private interview very often helps both the catechist and the learner to prevent a problem. Accept what the learner has to share and together try to arrive at a compatible solution. To attempt to correct each situation in the classroom or learning session itself becomes a distraction to the total group. Quite often this kind of correction becomes a shouting match between catechist and learner or an occasion of a "put-down" for one or the other.

If a problem continues with the student, arrange a conference with the parents and the student. When this kind of action is necessary, do not approach the conference in anger and disgust. Look at the positive side of the student as well as the negative aspect. Present the picture honestly and with clarity. Allow the student the opportunity to present his or her side of the story. Above all, let both parents and student know that, although you cannot accept inappropriate behavior, you do care for the student. It is this caring that has encouraged you to call the conference.

Problems may often arise because we have not taken the time necessary to prepare for our learners. Think about the materials you are presenting. Are the students involved in the process? Have you considered their skills and interests? Is the class alive or dead? Is the material practical, understandable, and related to their lived experience? Have you allowed the students time to evaluate the situation? Do you accept their suggestions and, where practical, apply them? Catechists must realize that the most effective time spent in their ministry is planning. When the students are creating problems and you have a situation of trying to cope with near anarchy, one of the first places to begin to look for a solution is at what *you* are doing.

Unfortunately there is no pill or tonic available for a catechist to take when trying to cope with students. We do not have available a miracle drug or any quick, instant, overnight solution to our problems. We enter the situation in faith, praying for God's wisdom that we may come to recognize and value the individuality and potential of each person we encounter. It is through this recognition that we enter learning situations prepared to deal with occasions of frustration and despair and equipped with the skills necessary to turn this situation into a fruitful learning experience.

QUESTIONS FOR REFLECTION

1. How much are your learners involved in the learning process itself?

2. If you are involved in child or adolescent catechesis, how will your relationship with the parents help you to deal properly with the child?

3. In what ways are you going to establish a student-catechist relationship?

_____
_____
_____
_____

5. CREATING A CONDUCIVE SETTING

People today are caught up in the never-ending job of decorating their homes. For some the job is pleasurable, but it requires time, planning, and detail. Decorating taste can be varied—modern, provincial (Italian or French), early American—while many simply look for the more functional-type furnishings with little regard to styling, mainly being interested in furniture serving its purpose. The setting we strive for, regardless of taste, talks about who we are. Above all, we are hopeful that our efforts will have a pleasant welcoming effect on our guests.

All catechists must become the decorator for their meeting place. The setting might be in a home. This could be the catechist's own home or the home of one of the people in the parish community. If the home is that of someone other than your own, you should visit with the person who was generous enough to offer its use. This visit would enable you to size up the adaptability and comfort of the area to be used.

Wherever the place for learning, the things which you should check out ahead of time are: restroom facilities, seating, blank wall for projection, work space for projects, the number that could be comfortably accommodated, clear directions to the home, clarification of expected time of arrival and departure of students, lighting, ventilation, and heating.

Perhaps your parish does not have any classrooms. In this case your catechetical classes may take place in the parish hall. Once again it is necessary to check out the facility. How many classes will be meeting at the same time? What specific area of the hall are you assigned to? Once this has been determined, look at your space. Are there electrical outlets for A-V materials? Do you have wall space for displays? Does the hall have portable blackboards, tables, chairs, and divider screens? What do you think the noise factor will be?

Maybe your setting will be the rooms used by the parochial school. Hopefully the school building will be looked upon as a shared facility to be used by the parochial school as well as the school of religion. If this is the situation, all users of the facility should understand the classroom as something shared by various members of the parish community. The maintenance of the classrooms should be shared by all the users. The various needs of each of the schools would have to be recognized to enable the goals to be met. Shared use of A-V materials, resources, and workshops as well as facilities is economically advantageous to the total parish community. Where such sharing does not exist, concerned parishioners should strive to make such sharing a reality. It would show on the part of the various programs a responsible attitude regarding parish finances and would serve to become a source of parish unity.

Take a minute and think about a time when you invited friends to your home for dinner. The occasion for the invitation is that you have some really good news to announce. You have planned the menu, taken some time in getting the place in order, dressed for the occasion, and enjoyed a quiet moment to think about how you were going to share the good news. Finally the doorbell rings. Your face lights up as you approach the door. You open it and enthusiastically greet your friends and in turn are greeted by them. You invite them in, and by your greeting they know that they are very welcome at your home.

In contrast, one of the most disappointing results of an invitation is to be invited and then ignored by the host and hostess. They were so involved in their own "thing" that they did not see you or were too busy at the time to greet you. After a short time you begin to wonder why you came. In fact, you may be spending your time thinking of ways to leave as politely and unnoticed as possible. Once able to make a successful escape, you will probably not accept another invitation from them for a long time.

A first priority for any catechist should be consideration of the learners. The setting should reflect this. Looking at a typical classroom given a catechist, many may feel that creating a conducive setting is an impossible task. It certainly is a challenge. Remembering so many of the classrooms that we have visited, we would have to say that not too many catechists have taken up the challenge.

Where do we start and what can we do? As a catechist you must, of course, resolve this for the unique situation in which you find yourself. A few suggestions may stimulate some ideas for you. Develop an area known as a "Prayer Corner" by placing a small table or stand in a corner of the room. On the table place a Bible, a candle, and a small vase for flowers. (Children in the primary grades would be responsible for bringing a flower each for the Prayer Corner. Older students generally are not so excited about this, so if you do not have access to flowers, you may want to substitute a small plant.) Have the students prepare a banner for the Prayer Corner. Depending on the age level you are working with, this banner could be as simple as butcher paper with pictures drawn, cut out, or pasted. These banners might follow the seasons of the Church calendar. A small rack could be added with magazines, religious stories, poetry, and some inexpensive Bibles. Adopt rules with the class as to how and when the Prayer Corner might be used—perhaps as the students complete an assignment and while waiting for the rest of the class to complete theirs. The Prayer Corner must always be used respectfully. The most important reminder about a Prayer Corner is that it is for the students and that they are responsible for maintaining it.

It is very important to display the work done by the students. At times and for many and varied reasons, space does not always seem available. As a suggestion obtain four cardboard boxes that fit compactly one into the other. Cover these boxes with contact paper. For classroom use place them pyramid-style in the classroom. Using straight pins, post the work of the students. This provides a colorful display for the students' work.

Small children can be seated very comfortably on the floor. This enables the catechist to be close to the group, thus offering security. Does your facility have this type of space? It is great for telling stories, using flannel boards, listening to a record, or talking to God. If it doesn't exist, the space can be provided by moving the furniture. If you are teaching in a classroom, perhaps you could number the desks with masking tape and markers to assure that you are able to put them in proper order for the next user of the facility.

Take time to acquaint the students with the room. Tell them what falls into the touchable area and what remains untouchable. This will not be foreign to the students. In their own homes they live daily with rules about what is theirs and what is not. If you take the time to deal adequately with this subject at the beginning of the year, it will go a long way toward peace and harmony for all concerned.

Either using poster paper or a bulletin board that is accessible in the room, begin to develop a collection of newspaper articles, pictures, or magazine articles that reflect the various themes of the textbook. Allow the students time to check it out as they arrive, during work on projects, or as they are leaving the class. Encourage the students to bring in items that they would like included on the bulletin board.

The way we care for materials tells a great deal about how the students will use them. If books, scissors, pencils, paste, paper, etc., are used by the students, did you take time to see that they were in good condition when given to the students? If you are careless about what has been given to the students, rest assured that your students will be as careless about their use and the work they are expected to accomplish.

All catechists must be responsible in the preparation of their classrooms. Last-minute preparation of the classroom is inexcusable and will ultimately lead not only to your disenchantment but also to a negative reaction on the part of the students. You should always arrive thirty minutes to an hour ahead of time. This allows for setting up, reviewing what is to be done, and arranging the materials. At the time the students are expected to arrive, you should be at the door to meet and greet each student with a warm hello and a smile. Classes should be sufficiently planned so that you are free at dismissal time to say good-bye to each of the students as they depart or to respond to questions that a particular student might have and did not have clarified during the class.

It may seem that a great deal of time and work is devoted to setting a conducive atmosphere. But when such a mood is created, the learners are implicitly being told that what you and they are doing is important. And what is more important than communicating the Word of God?

QUESTIONS FOR REFLECTION

1. What needs to be changed in your catechetical setting to make it more conducive to learning?

2. Which of the above can you take care of yourself?_____

3. Whom should you see to effect the other changes?_____

6. PARENT INVOLVEMENT

An integral element of the catechesis of children and youth is the involvement of the parents. The National Catechetical Directory very clearly calls for all programs of catechesis to include the participation of the parents:

> Though the influence of peers and of adult catechists is important, catechetical programs are not intended to supplant parents as the primary educators of their children. Parental involvement in catechetical programs is essential (n. 229).

Throughout the history of the Church, parents have always been regarded as the primary educators of their children. This is not a new and radical change on the part of the Church; however, it calls on each of us involved in catechesis to recall our own history to see what happened to downplay the role of the parents. Why do we as educators and parents often feel that it is the sole responsibility of the Church to make our children Catholic?

Parochial schools were established for Catholics of the United States in the nineteenth century. Communities of religious women and men founded and operated schools for the orphans and the poor children of the recently arrived imigrant Catholics to enable the children to be properly assimilated into the American culture and prepared for meaningful employment without losing their Catholic heritage. With the growth of the public school system, parochial schools were seen as protecting the children from the secularizing influence of the public schools. During the twentieth century, based on the success of the parochial school system, each diocese conducted extensive building programs and encouraged many communities of religious women and men to staff them and take over the catechetical needs of its children. Through the middle of the twentieth century the parochial school system grew and prospered. It was one of the real success stories of the American Catholic Church.

Parents, being concerned with working, raising families, and trying to adapt to an ever-changing world with all its technological advancements, were quite comfortable with the system. Parishes strove to create schools large enough to accommodate every Catholic boy and girl. Pastors very emphatically told parents of the grave obligation they had to provide a Catholic education for their children. "Catholic education" was translated to mean: "Send your child to our parish school." As a result, the catechesis of our children came to be seen as something that only Father, Sister, or Brother could do. Unintentional though it may have been, the consequence was that parents abdicated their role as the primary educators of their children in the Catholic religion.

Due to overcrowded classrooms in the parish school, parents' inability to pay tuition, or simply the desire of parents to enroll their children in the public school, parishes began to realize that there were many children not attending their school but who needed religious instruction. Through the Confraternity of Christian Doctrine parishioners devoted generous amounts of time as catechists to provide instruction for the public school children. Again the parents turned over the responsibility of the catechetical preparation of their children to the "Church."

Today more and more talk is being heard in Church circles about parent involvement. Many attempts have been made with a variety of models: parent education programs, family catechesis, "do-it-yourself" programs, etc. Sometimes the news is exciting. However, quite often we hear from parochial school and school of religion programs some bleak responses: "Parents aren't interested." "We aren't supported by the parents." "Parents don't understand what we are teaching their children." "The only way we can even get them to a meeting is by threatening them." The groundwork that was laid for the parochial school system and CCD system without parental involvement did not just happen overnight. It took years of labor by dedicated persons and the support of responsible people in the Church. To rethink, devise, and implement programs of parent involvement will also take time. Before roots will take and the fuits of our labors become acceptable, it will require the same type of labor with the support of responsible people in the Church.

How To Begin. Invitation is the key. When people are invited to participate in anything, they come with an open attitude, whereas *mandating* their presence gives more assurance of their *physical* presence but often leaves a great deal to be desired in their *personal* presence. Knowing what they would enjoy is of prime importance. This would entail taking some sort of needs assessment of the group. We must recognize that they have already been places. Our task is to encourage them to move with us. If we are sincere in our invitation, we will prepare them for an enjoyable and worthwhile experience.

Think about those we invite to our homes. We are concerned about their comfort and make sure that things are prepared accordingly. We extend hospitality and try to center our discussions on topics of interest to them. When we have received invitations from boring people, we usually make excuses and try to decline the invitation. As catechists we do not want to be boring for these parents. Therefore, we have to think about areas of common interest in which we could explore together. In our catechetical programs that common interest would of course include our students, their children. Centering the purpose of our invitation on our relationship with their child and on their relationship with their child, we have set a climate of mutual interest and have somewhere to go.

Sacramental preparation is a golden opportunity to work with parents and students together. In this area you will find a particularly diverse group of people. Many will not understand why sacraments are different from what they were when these parents were children. Some will not even know what sacraments are. However, this is not a time to be judgmental. It is rather a time of opening up people, growing and sharing together. When one thinks about some of the typical comments often made by catechists after one of these parent meetings for sacramental preparation, one clearly begins to understand how parents are made to feel: "What can you expect? They haven't crossed the doorway of a church in ten years." "They can't receive Communion; marriage problems, you know." "That kid doesn't know her prayers. But it's no wonder. Look at the parents!" All of these are "killer" statements and, above all, not Christian.

Parents' Orientation Day. This would be an opportunity for the catechist and the parents to meet prior to the opening of school. It would be that time when catechists can share something about themselves and their interest in assisting the parents in the catechesis of their children. The National Catechetical Directory mentions that any textbook used in catechetical programs for children should include "manuals or developed notes for parents" (n. 264). Orientation Day would be an ideal time for the catechists or the persons responsible for the program to explain the parents' section of the text and how the the parents' material, properly used, will assist both parents and catechists in attaining their mutual goals. Information could be given about the operation of school, times, holidays, behavior, etc. Parents should have an opportunity to ask questions or clarify concerns. They could be assured that their input is not only sought but is necessary for the operation of the program.

Very often when a child comes home from catechetical instruction, the mother will ask: "What did you do in class today, David?" David replies, "Nothing." A parents' meeting would go a long way to dispel doubts of the effectiveness of the program for David's mother. Mother would be very much aware of what David was expected to do in class and would have the information necessary to enter into a discussion with him.

Pre-School Programs. Concentration on parents with children in pre-school programs is a great source of future catechists and aides for catechetical programs. The parents are involved in the process of unfolding God in the lives of their small children. They participate with the catechists in the operation of the pre-school program. Stand outside any pre-school program and watch the proud and happy parents of an exuberant child. You will recognize at once the joy and love of the parents and the child. They have encountered catechesis in its initial stages. With the right encouragement and motivation, they can and will continue their involvement. People tend to be shy when it comes to getting involved in catechesis. Your encouragement is necessary; your invitation is vital.

The most important facet of getting parents involved is acceptance. All of us have our own history. In our journey we have taken many roads. Some have been fortunate enough to have been made aware of what has been taking place in the Church over the years. Others, not quite so fortunate, have not had the opportunity to share this journey. For large numbers in the Church, catechesis ceased at the reception of the sacraments. We have to be open to these people. We must recognize them as loved by the same God who loves us all. It is our responsibility to meet them where they are, respond to their needs, and strive always to help them develop an ever-deepening relationship with the Lord. In accepting this challenge, each of us will be enriched, and we will continue to grow in faith.

> Jesus' words, "You are my friends if you do what I command you" (Jn 15:14), point to the fact that the life of faith involves a relationship, a friendship, between persons. As the quality of a friendship between human beings is affected by such things as their maturity and freedom, their knowledge of each other, and the manner and frequency of their communication, so the quality of a friendship with God is affected by the characteristics of the human party. Because people are capable of continual development, so are their relationships with God. Essentially, development in faith is the process by which one's relationship with the Father becomes more like Jesus' (cf. Jn 14:6f); it means becoming more Christlike. This is not just a matter of subjective, psychological change, but involves establishing and nurturing a real relationship to Jesus and the Father in the Holy Spirit, through a vigorous sacramental life, prayer, study, and serving others (NCD, n.173).

QUESTIONS FOR REFLECTION

1. Considering that the parents are indeed the primary educators of their child, how do you as a catechist see your relationship with the parent in working together to deepen the child's faith life?_____

_____
_____
_____
_____

2. How can parents become actively involved in the catechesis of their child without a mandated program of parent education?_____

_____
_____

3. Sacraments are seen by the Church as a teachable moment. How can you as a catechist make it a teachable moment for the family as well as the child?

Unit Three

PROCESSES FOR LEARNING

1. ADAPTATION OF MATERIALS FOR THE STUDENT

Most of us at one time or another have taken a small child to a restaurant for dinner and found that the chairs at the table are much too low for the child to eat comfortably. The waiter asks if we would like a high chair or a riser for the child. Placed in it the child is now able to reach the table comfortably. An adaptation has been made to enable the child to take part in the meal.

Adapting materials in a catechetical setting is also necessary to allow the students to take part. Like the child in the restaurant, unable to eat comfortably until the chair was adapted, the students' participation only becomes possible when the catechist has digested the materials and devised ways to adapt the lesson to the needs and developmental stages of the learner.

Suppose, for a moment, that your lesson would entail an introduction to the Gospel. The teacher's guide might suggest that each student be given a copy of the New Testament. By knowing your students you would be aware that the majority of the students have little knowledge of Scripture, while at the same time the suggested lessons are calling for an understanding of authorship and inspiration. The language used would be new to the students. As a result, they would have difficulty understanding the concept. The suggested medium in the text is ROA filmstrip series, "Understanding Scripture: A Gospel Portrait of Jesus," episode #6. In viewing the filmstrip you find that the message is beyond the abilities of the learners. In order to present the lesson, you must begin to adapt the materials if you are to make the lesson relevant to the learners.

To begin, you could share with the students some item of good news that has happened in your life—perhaps something that has taken place in the local community or parish community. This could be followed by asking the students to write a statement about some "good news" that has happened to them that they would like to share. After this is accomplished, you could talk about the Gospel as "good news." The word "Gospel" means "good news." We refer to the Gospel according to Matthew, Mark, Luke, and John as the "good news." These four men would be understood as the authors of these four accounts of the Gospel (good news). These writings are a reflection of their experience of Jesus (directly or indirectly) and the recording of these experiences under the guidance (inspiration) of the Holy Spirit.

In previewing the filmstrip which deals with authorship and inspiration, you might take the script and rephrase the script to fit the ability of the students to understand. Rather than using the record or cassette, you could use your rephrased script as the filmstrip was being viewed. Perhaps only a few frames of the filmstrip would be sufficient to convey that portion of the message relevant to the lesson. This would be an appropriate adaptation of the materials for the needs of the learners.

Quite often with children the language of Scripture is beyond their ability to comprehend. Aware of this difficulty, you would take the Scripture passage and rewrite it in language understood by your students.

Many programs operate without the availability of media which were suggested in the teacher's guide. You often are called to be creative in your ability to adapt to the situation. A series of picture postures, carefully selected and presented, can be as effective as the media in presenting the lesson.

Singing is a gift which some of us have and in which others are totally lacking. Those who cannot sing are able to adapt by using records and cassettes or perhaps by looking for a person who can sing and who would be willing to help in the class.

Often you will find that your learners have difficulties in reading or writing. The lesson may call for students to read material or to respond in writing to a particular statement or series of questions that you feel they would not be able to deal with. Aware of this, you could present the material phrased in ways that they can understand and form the students into groups of four or five to discuss the information you have communicated.

Perhaps your lesson deals with the life of a particular saint. The text has a story that you are to read. However, if you are aware that your students do not enjoy listening to something being read to them, you could take the story, write it in the form of a play, and have the students act out the story.

You must always be aware of your learners in order to adapt materials. Most catechetical programs deal with students who have attended structured classroom situations five days a week. If as a catechist you expect to continue this structure into the sixth day or after six hours of class, you will generally find it difficult for the students to enter in. Much adaptation is needed as you become aware of the attitudes, skills, and abilities of the learners. In knowing the material that is to be presented and in making the correct choice as to how you are going to present the lesson, you will be able to adapt readily, easily, and comfortably and be more assured of the students' ability to participate.

2. PROJECTS FOR VARIOUS AGE LEVELS

PRIMARY LEVEL (GRADES 1-3)

1. Reproduce copies of a bare tree. This can be done on ditto masters. Reproduce copies of leaves. This also can be done on ditto masters. Ask the students to take home the paper with the leaves and have their parents help them with the names of grandparents, aunts, uncles, cousins, mother, father, brothers and sisters. Have them print the names of each person and the child's relationship to each one on separate leaves. In class have them take the copy of the bare tree and, after cutting out the leaves, have them paste the leaves on the tree. This would then become the student's "Family Tree." You can design a class around our specialness as members of God's family.

2. Make a pattern of a boy and a girl. Have each student trace the pattern according to his or her sex. Have them color the figure with washable markers or crayons and color the hair, eyes, etc., so that it would represent themselves. Divide the class into groups of five to seven students. Give each group a coat hanger and some colorful yarn. Have the students make a mobile for their group. (Alternatives to a coat hanger would be wooden dowel or tree branches.) This could be used as a project on community, and the finished product would represent the total class.

Similarly, one could have the students trace the number of persons needed for their family. Have each student bring a coat hanger to class. The students would then be able to decorate the figures to represent the members of their family. Each student would then have an individual mobile that could be taken home and shared with other members of the family

3. *Thanksgiving.* Prepare a large poster or bulletin board in a bright autumn color for the background. Cut out of heavy poster board a large cornucopia. Have the children select a pattern of a variety of fruits or vegetables and cut it out of the appropriately colored construction paper. Now have the students write their own thoughts of thankfulness for parents, teachers, school, Church, God, freedom, etc.

4. *"Lend a Hand" Bulletin Board.* In sharing with your students the many ways Jesus touched the lives of others, explain that you are going to give them an opportunity to be like Jesus and touch others. Every time they lend a hand to another person, give them a copy of a hand that has been traced and cut out of light construction paper. On this hand they write the way they helped the other person and sign their name. This is then placed on the "Lend a Hand" bulletin board. For the younger students who are not yet proficient in printing many words, they can take the hand home and have their parents or an older brother or sister help them write their message. They print or write their own name, return it to the teacher, and then it is placed on the bulletin board.

5. Using the book *Stories by Jesus* by Rev. John Behnke (Paulist Press, 1977), rewrite the stories for role-playing by the students. The book is easily adapted to role-playing. It offers a variety of stories that will fit quite well into your religion classes. Your class can perform this play for another class or perhaps for the primary department. It would be excellent to have your students put on this play for the parents at Open House.

6. Have a picture of Jesus and friend traced on a ditto master. Use only one half of the ditto for the picture. On the bottom half, have the students write their story of what they would have to say to Jesus if they were the person in the picture with him.

7. Give each student a strip of colorful construction paper. This should be cut approximately 1" x 12" in length. In the center of the strip, each should print his or her name. In a class on unity the catechist could then move around the class and staple the strips together forming a chain. A chain is a sign of strength, togetherness, and unity. The catechist can point out to the class that alone each

of us is special, but together, working, praying, and doing things we become ever so much more special.

8. *Diorama.* Have each student bring a shoe box to class. Have the students trace from patterns or cut out pictures from magazines that would represent their church, school, or home as well as their friends. Have them color or paint the inside of the box on all sides representing the sky, trees, grass, streets, mountains, etc. Now have them paste the figures they have cut out in the box. The outside of the box can be painted or covered with wallpaper or construction paper. This is an ideal project when you are working on the units concerned with community. It shows that they are members of the parish community, school community, and family community and that they have their own community of friends.

9. Have the students prepare a model city. Using a table as the base, have the students collect small boxes of various sizes and shapes. These boxes can be covered and designed to represent supermarkets, service stations, police department, fire department, hospitals, churches, schools, houses, etc. Using pieces of shrubbery, gravel, small pebbles and the like, have them build roads and design their city. When the work is done you might then elect city officers, e.g. mayor, council members, fire chief, etc. You might have them develop the rules that will be needed to operate the city for the safety and well-being of each resident. The use of this project is broad and will fit into many areas of your course of studies.

In all of these projects do allow the students' work to be visible. Each of us is artistic and creative and capable of doing great things. Let us begin to allow and encourage our students to get involved and accept their responsibility in completing class projects. Our job will be well done when we are able to assist them in carrying the project to completion. Any project that becomes "my project" is soon dropped by the students. If it is their project, they have a vested interest and will do their best to see that it is a project worth viewing.

INTERMEDIATE LEVEL (GRADES 4-6)

1. *Presenting the Commandments.* Have the class write letters to the mayor of the city, council members, city treasurer, etc. In the letters they might ask why and how laws are formed for the city. As elected representatives of the people these persons are charged with the responsibility of the safety and welfare of the citizens. Laws are enacted to guarantee it.

```
   CLASS                CLASS
   OFFICERS             RULES

Pres. David          1. To be kind
V. Pres. Norrida        to all persons
Sec. Julia           2. To be respon-
Treas. Armando          sible for my
                        actions
Moderator            3. To allow
  Miss Sanchez          others to
                        differ with me
```

Commandments are God's law. They also speak of the safety and welfare of all people. Using the letters received from the elected officials of the city, you will have a basis to begin a study of commandments or Church laws.

This project could involve the electing of class officers by the students and the formulation of laws (rules) that they accept for the benefit of the "citizens" (students) in your class.

2. *Welcome/Getting To Know You.* Have each student in the class trace his or her footprint on light colored construction paper. Have the students cut out their footprint and give them the opportunity to write their own summer journey. When they have had time to complete their sharing, have them turn the footprint to the reverse side and write the various ways they showed others during their summer journey that they are followers of Jesus. These could then be pasted on butcher paper for use as an altar covering for a liturgy or prayer celebration at a later time.

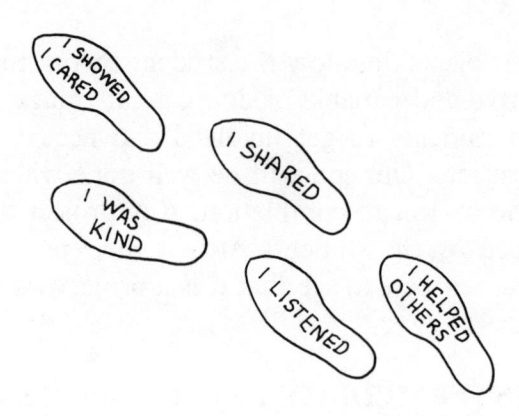

3. *Old Testament Study.* As the student is introduced to the Old Testament, the catechist can present the Scriptures as a journey of the Israelite people. Pick up on the theme of journey and for your class project have each student prepare his or her travelogue/travel folder. Allow the students to design their folder based on the lesson that they are working on. Allow them to express both in art form (drawing, collages, cartoon, etc.) and in writing their response to the lesson presented. A written statement at the bottom of each paper of the travel folder will enable the catechist to see how well the lesson was understood on the part of the student. These travel folders would be great to share with parents of students or other catechists in the program.

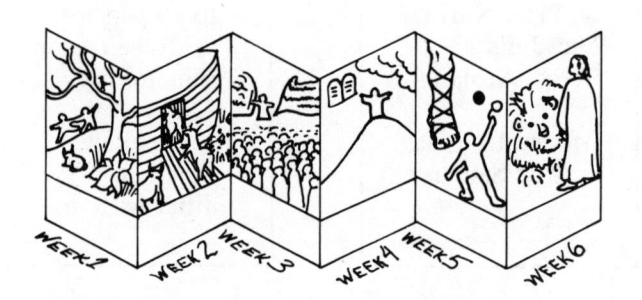

4. *Sacramental Review.* On this level catechetical textbooks generally include a review of sacraments. The catechist can present to the students an opportunity to prepare their own newspaper. (This can be a class project or one done on an individual basis with each child preparing his or her own newspaper.) As each of the sacraments comes up in the text, the catechist can ask the students to write an article of their understanding of that particular sacrament. For those sacraments received by the child, the catechist can ask the students to write the article as an eyewitness of the action that took place. These articles could include their preparation, the ceremony, people present at the celebration or even their own personal understanding of what they were participating in at the time. They would then be encouraged in light of the new information received in their review to research and write articles about sacraments as reflected in the Church today. Various forms of art work could be used to enhance the newspaper. This newspaper could be compiled over the number of weeks in which the students are par-

ticipating in the sacramental review. The newspaper would be an excellent display and conversation piece for parent meetings.

5. *Mary, the Mother of God.* Presenting Mary to students can very often be confusing to them. An outstanding quality of Mary was her unquestioning *"yes"* to God. Her life is a model for each of us whether adult or child. Mary's great trust in the Father to bring her to perfect happiness and her total belief in God's love for her are reminders to each of us of great value. Using a large poster board, print letters for a phrase such as: "Like Mary, I also respond to God by...." Ask the students how they say "yes" to God in their lives. As they think through in order to answer, pass out cut-out flowers (made from construction paper) in various shades. Have them write on the flowers the way they have responded with a "yes" to God. When they have had an opportunity to write their thoughts, have them come to the front of the room and prayerfully repeat their "yes" for the total class. Then have them paste their flower on one of the stems that you have drawn on the poster board. You could then use this poster as part of a prayer celebration on Mary as your theme.

6. *Beatitudes.* The catechist should look for words that would allow the students to find meaning to the message of the Beatitudes. Much of the language of the Scriptures is difficult for the students of this age level to understand, and the message is lost. Take a look at the Beatitudes from *The Stories of Jesus.* Tell the story as rewritten by Father Behnke to the students. Allow time for the students to ask questions about the message. You might encourage them by asking if they understood the story. After you have discussed the story, divide the class into eight groups, giving each group a poster board with the caption of one of

the Beatitudes printed at the top of the poster board. In their small groups have them make a collage of the particular Beatitude you have assigned to their group. They can use articles or headlines from newspapers and pictures from magazines, or they can write or draw their own thoughts and ideas which express how the Beatitudes are being lived out by people today. Allow each group to share its poster. In concluding the class you might ask each student to write a paragraph or two on how each personally is a Beatitude person.

7. *Journal.* The catechist can use lined notebook paper, construction paper for the cover, and yarn, brads or staples to bind individual journals for each student. Have a contest on the designing of the cover of the journal. Ask the students to design the cover of their journal so that it would reflect who they are as a person. Have a group of older students or other catechists judge the journal covers. Give awards (first, second, and third prize). This journal can then be used by the students to write their thoughts or reflections on the weekly lessons.

```
People of Old Testament
a. Sampson      Sarah
b. Adam         Gomer
c. Hosea        Eve
d. Cain         Ruth
e. Naomi        Delilah
f. Abraham      Abel
Match the above names by
drawing connecting lines
```

8. *Matching Game.* Using the various people of the Old Testament that the students have discovered on the journey, prepare a matching game. This game will enable catechists to see how well they have presented the materials. On a ditto master type two columns using the names of people from the Scriptures. This can be done on an individual basis or by allowing the students to work in teams. At this age level the students are quite ready and pleased to work at team effort.

JUNIOR HIGH LEVEL (GRADES 7-8)

1. *Traits of Jesus That I Admire.* Junior high students have through their intermediate years admired many persons. At this particular time in their lives they often cover over their lifelong heroes to be acceptable to their peer group and one with them. Help them to reflect on the heroes of past years and to recall the ways they tried to imitate these persons. This could be written or discussed in small groups. You might start by sharing with them those people you admired during the years you were in junior high school. What was the music and dance craze of your particular era? What was the world scene at that time? Who were the prophets of that era? Allow the students to take some quiet time to reflect

about Jesus. Give them copies of the good news and have them search the Scriptures for qualities or traits they admire about Jesus. Have them write in their journal the trait or the qualities they admire the most, citing book, chapter, and verse from which they found their information. Conclude by preparing a prayer celebration including the qualities and traits they admired and discovered in the Scriptures.

2. *Problem-Solving Clinic.* Cover a shoe box that will become the place where the students are permitted to write problems they face in their daily life. These are placed by the student in the box with no names given. When time permits, the catechist will share one or more of the problems with the total class. Together they will work on ways to solve the particular problem. Catechists need not be the persons with every solution. At the same time they should assist the students in arriving at a reasonable solution to the problem. Good judgment on the part of the catechist must be used in determining which of those problems submitted are capable of being solved by the group.

3. *Prayer.* Junior high students are quite capable of deep prayerfulness. This is most often quiet and not easily shared with their peer group. At the same time they often turn to the Father at moments of crisis in their lives. The catechist should allow the students to prepare a "Prayer Box" that is always available to them. Encourage them to write their prayer (without names) and put them into the prayer box. During your prayer session of the class, include one or more of the students' prayers as part of the class prayer.

4. *Unity.* As a sign of unity ask the students in your class to write a letter or design a card for the parochial school student or school of religion (CCD) student, whatever the case may be, with whom they share a desk. The catechist can set the example by writing a note or preparing a card for the person with whom he or she shares the room. The students might share information like name, age, grade, school they attend, and material they are working with in their religion class. They might also say how the two share a common affiliation together in the same parish community.

5. *Helping Others: Service.* Assist the students in seeing how fortunate they are in their own lives. They are surrounded by persons who care for them and give them support. Often the student is resentful of this direction or caring. This resentment most often occurs in surface responses. Ask for a person from one of the detention facilities to come to speak to the students. Have that person talk about life in these facilities and give profiles of the youths locked up there. This will often lead students to grow in their appreciation of family members. As a response to this talk, have the students earn money and purchase gifts that can be given to the detention facility for distribution to the young persons detained there. (These gifts could include books, games, toiletry articles, writing paper, etc.)

6. *Responsible Members of the Parish Community.* Working with students of this level the catechist becomes aware quite rapidly how little students feel about being a part of the parish community. Meet with the pastor, associate pastor, liturgy committee, or whoever handles the various responsibilities. Ask if they could set aside a weekend when the junior high students could fill the roles of

lector, usher, servers, gift bearers at the offertory procession, and perhaps even musicians for the celebration. This could be done at each of the scheduled Masses on a weekend. A great deal of effort would need to be done on the part of the catechist, as well as the students, to assure a smooth operation, but the experience is well worth the effort and can be a really meaningful experience for the students.

    7. *Sacramental Review.* Ask the students to respond in writing: "How can you prove you are really a member of the family that you live with?" You will receive many types of responses: "I saw a copy of my birth certificate." "My mother told me about it." Now ask how they could make others believe if they did not have another person to assist them in proving they were members of a particular family or if they did not have legal documents to prove the point. One way is to look at our own personal history. "What events from the time you were small children can you recall that will help you verify your story?" In recalling they will talk about a variety of ways. Some might recall that they have older or younger brothers and sisters, grandparents, etc. They might remember special family celebrations they attended, such as Christmas, birthdays, anniversaries, and First Communion. They might think of that first day of school and their teachers they had over the years. Or perhaps they remember the different places where they have lived. Using these stories as a basis, the catechist can begin to discuss baptism as that special time when parents ask the Church to baptize their child as a member of the Christian community. They can explore the Eucharist as nourishment to enable the students to live their lives, giving witness and growing in relationship with the Father. Confirmation is seen as that time when a person is strengthened in that relationship and willingness to serve others as part of that witness. Each of the sacraments received and lived by us is tied to our own personal histories as members of God's loved family. Because the students have had the opportunity to think of their family history, they will be in touch with the why of their participation in sacraments. Misconceptions can be straightened out at this time by the catechist.

    8. *Getting To Know You.* Catechists really have to know the students they are working with. Each student comes from various backgrounds and has been in a process of formation for a good number of years. Prepare a questionnaire and ask each student to respond. Tell the students that the information is not going to be shared, that it is for your own personal use in trying to make the class as interesting as possible. To assure that the information will not be shared, you might suggest that the students not write their names on the questionnaire.

QUESTIONS (YOU MIGHT ASK)

    1. What is the one activity you enjoy most?_____
_____
_____
_____
_____

2. What is your favorite kind of reading? (a) Historical (b) Biographies (c) Mysteries (d) Other_____

3. How many years have you attended religion (catechetical) classes?_____

4. What is it that you would most like to know about the "Church"?_____

5. If you had the opportunity to have a dream come true, what would be your dream?_____

6. What do you think the major problem is in the world today?_____

7. What do you see as signs of hope in the world today?_____

193

8. How do you see yourself serving others? _____
_____
_____
_____